£5.99
8A
wk 26

Railways of India

Jan B Young

Railways of India

Jan B Young

Copyright © 2020 by Jan B Young
All Rights Reserved

ISBN 978-1-716-89551-7

Cover: Chhatrapati Shivaji Maharaj Terminus was built in 1888 to commemorate Queen Victoria's Golden Jubilee. Known as Victoria Terminal until its name was changed in 1996, it still serves the city of Bombay with eighteen platforms. [Author collection]

Table of Contents

Introduction

The five Napoleonic Wars, fought between 1803 and 1815, resulted in the relative impoverishment of France and Germany and the relative wealth of England. As a result, the English (and, to a lesser degree, the Americans) had the opportunity to invest in technology when competing nations didn't. One result was the early development of steam power in Britain and the use of that steam power to advance Britain's imperial ambitions. The world's first railroad (the Stockton & Darlington in County Durham, England some two hundred miles north of London) first ran in 1825 and the first in the USA (the B&O in Baltimore, Maryland) in 1830.

Prior to the opening of the Suez Canal in 1869, travel between Britain and India required a lengthy trip around Cape Horn, often taking between four and six months to accomplish under sail. By one estimate as few as two hundred people did it as passengers each year. When the Suez Canal opened, things got a lot easier. With the resources of India available for the taking and with the transportation problem much reduced, the British moved in and began to seriously invest in the country.

The area of the United States (the lower 48 states) is about 3.1 million square miles. In the nineteenth century (before Pakistan was cut away), India was about 1.6 million square miles or about half as big. The distance from Chicago to Oakland, California as the crow flies is about 1,850 miles while the distance from Mumbai to Kolkata (Bombay to Calcutta) is just over a thousand miles, also approximately half as big. By the mid-1970s, India Railways had over thirty-seven thousand miles of line and, except for the Soviet Union, was the largest system in the world under a single management. While the USA has more route-miles, it is divided among eight major Class I railroads and a large number of smaller, Class II and Class III lines.

The geology of India is, in many respects, not conducive to the building of railroads. The west is largely filled with mountains; the Thal Ghat and Bhore Ghat passes through the Sahyadri and Western Ghat ranges along the coast are backed up by the Vindhya Range, all with peaks as high as four thousand feet, made of the hardest impregnable rock and seamed with deep valleys. But what's more, the mountains of India are not cold and dry like those of the USA and Canada, they are clad with jungle and filled with wild beasts, dangerous reptiles and voracious insects.

Construction of the Bhore Ghat Incline took eight years. It involved twenty-five tunnels, eight substantial masonry viaducts, the removal of 554 million cubic feet of hard rock and the placement of 67.5 million cubic feet of fill. Workers drilled holes for black powder explosives while hanging from cliffs on ropes much as Chinese workers did in the Sierras when the Central Pacific was being built.

In the East, India is relatively flat but is cut with broad, highly variable and dangerous rivers requiring many crossings. The Hooghly, the Brahmaputra, the Padma, the Ganges, the Jamuna, the Mahanadi, the Narbada, the Godavari and dozens of tributaries all stand in the way. Most of these rivers flow through vast areas of flatland and flood seasonally over huge areas, often changing course as they go. What is a trickle in the dry season becomes a massive flood in the wet. Therefore bridging had to be extensive and had to be strong enough to resist the worst of the floods even though they only occurred briefly each year. Ironwork for the early bridges was made in Britain but caissons, foundation work and assembly was all local.

By 1971 the Indian Railways had over a hundred thousand bridges, essentially all either stone, iron or steel. Unlike early bridges in the USA, wood construction was rare and, because suitable clay for brick-making was hard to find in India, the use of brick was limited to portions of the country. But bridges were numerous and, especially in the east, long. The Upper Sone Bridge, opened on February 22, 1900, was 10,052 feet long. The Dufferin Bridge over the Ganges, opened in 1887, was a half-mile long.

Mark Twain traveled extensively in India and wrote:

> Curious rivers they are; low shores a dizzy distance apart with nothing between but an enormous acreage of sand-flats with sluggish little veins of water dribbling around amongst them; Saharas of sand, small-pox-pitted with footprints punctured in belts as straight as the equator clear from the one shore to the other – a dry-shod ferry, you see. Long railway bridges are required for this sort of rivers, and India has them. You approach Allahabad by a very long one. It was now carrying us across the bed of the Jumna, a bed which did not seem to have been slept in for one while or more. It wasn't all river-bed – most of it was overflow ground.

In the north, there are more rivers and deep canyons to be crossed and there is also waterless desert country, all building up to the base of the incredible Himalayas. And this is overlaid with weather patterns that bring torrential rains and the extreme heat of the tropics including the occasional cyclone. In December 1964, near the village of Dhanushkodi on India's southeast coast, a passenger train was caught in an unexpected storm and was washed out to sea with between one and two hundred people on board. Although the locomotive and cars were later found, only a handful of people survived. Nearby, a relatively unusual 1914 Scherzer rolling lift bridge survived but its approaches were heavily damaged and it was out of service for forty-six days.

And the country is beset with earthquakes, particularly in the mountainous areas in the north, east and west. The earthquakes are caused by movement of the Indian tectonic plate into the Asian plate at about the rate of forty-seven millimeters or two inches per year.

Disease was also a barrier to construction in the nineteenth century: cholera, pneumonia, typhoid, smallpox and malaria all played a part along with something called kala-azar (also known as blackwater fever). Disease was caused, at least in part, by the unsanitary conditions the laborers lived in.

On the other hand, the demand for transportation was very much present. In 1831 a mail cart service took forty-eight hours to make the hundred-mile journey from Bombay to Poona at a cost of ninety Rupees per passenger.

India has always been a blend of the Hindu and Muslim religions. The concept of pilgrimage is important in both so there has long been significant demand for travel from all classes of life to visit sacred sites. The Muslim hajj, a visit to the holy city of Mecca, is reflected in the Hindu Kumbha Melas in which one of four pilgrimage sites hosts a gathering every three years. Seventeen million attended the Kumbha Mela at Prayag (Allahabad) in 2001 and many of those arrived and departed by train; an estimated thirty million attended in 2013.

In addition to the pilgrimages, there are massive religious festivals that are made possible by the railways, draw hundreds of thousands of participants. At least half of them arrive by train, stay anywhere from a day to a week, and then return, again by train. Elaborate arrangements are required for sanitation, security, booking and checking of tickets, and planning for the arrival and departure of trains and there are dozens, if not hundreds, of these festivals each year for Hindus, Buddhists, Muslims, Sikhs, Parsis, and Christians.

In 1928, by one count, there were five hundred twenty events in India with an attendance of ten thousand or more and thirty-seven of them had attendance of a hundred thousand or more. The Kumbha Mela at Hardwar in 1927 required 143 inward and 206 outward special trains on the single-track Hardwar branch. A total of 620,000 passengers were carried over a ten-day period. One is reminded of the 1926 Eucharistic Congress held in Chicago that attracted a half-million attendees and of the annual Army-Navy football games that filled a Pennsylvania Railroad freight yard with special trains for the duration of the game, but all on a vastly greater scale.

By the 1950s, the gross annual revenue of the Indian Railways (by then almost entirely nationalized) amounted to three-fifths of the gross annual revenue of the government. The railways were one of the largest nationalized enterprises in the world.

In 2017 the Indian Railways was the fourth largest railway network in the world with a route length of 67,368 kilometers or 41,861 miles. About half of the routes were electrified and a third of them were double or multi-tracked. In the year ending March 2018, the Indian Railways carried 8.26 billion passengers and transported 1.16 billion tons of freight. In that same year, the Indian Railways were projected to have revenue of 1.874 trillion Rupees (US$26 billion) and an operating ratio of 96.0 percent. The Indian Railway ran more than 20,000 passenger trains daily on both long-distance and suburban routes from 7,349 stations across India. The most common types of trains ran at an average speed of 50.6 kilometers per hour (31.4 miles per hour) while premium passenger trains like the Rajdhani Express and the Shatabdi Express ran at peak speed of 140–150 kilometers per hour (87–93 miles per hour), the Gatiman Express between New Delhi and Jhansi touched a peak speed of 160 kilometers per hour (99 miles per hour) and the Vande Bharat (also known as Train-18) between Delhi-Varanasi and Delhi-Katra reached 180 kilometers per hour (110 miles per hour). As of March 2017, rolling stock consisted of 277,987 freight cars, 70,937 passenger coaches and 11,452 locomotives. The Indian Railway owns locomotive and coach-production facilities at several locations. The world's eighth-largest employer, it had 1.30 million employees as of March 2016.

Although not totally true, the India Railways are mostly isolated with few rail links between India and neighboring countries. Trains to and from Pakistan are operated and cancelled from time to time based on political tensions between the two nations. Four weekly trains run into Bangladesh and service into Nepal is provided over two lines. No rail link exists with Myanmar but one is under construction. None connect India with either China or Sri Lanka.

Rudyard Kipling, Mark Twain, and George Orwell all wrote about the Indian Railways and it is amusing to see what they said on the subject.

- Kipling's *The Man Who Would Be King* (1888) begins with the meeting of an Englishman and an Indian vagabond on the road from Mhow to Ajmer in an otherwise-empty intermediate class car. Kipling describes the intermediate class as being "very awful indeed" with no cushions. Kipling notes that in hot weather intermediate-class passengers are taken out of the carriages dead and in all weathers they are looked down upon.
- Mark Twain, in his *Following the Equator* (1896) describes the uniquely-Indian custom of arriving at the depot a day or two before departure and simply camping out on the platform. He describes people sleeping, washing, cooking, scrubbing laundry, and doing all the necessary parts of life while waiting for the train. He also describes the impact of the caste system and the fact that the railways acted to force together people of different castes who wouldn't otherwise have come within miles of each other. (Another writer observed that many third and fourth-class passengers came from a life and a village where time wasn't measured and thus had little or no concept of a schedule.)
- Twain goes on to describe his accommodations on the train and to remark at how inexpensive travel was for him. He also describes the Indian first-come-first-served sleeper arrangements, the need for the traveler to provide his/her own bedding, and the complications that ensue.
- Twain rode on the East Indian Railway from Calcutta and described the journey as "comfortable." He also rode the Darjeeling Himalayan two foot gauge and described it as "infinitely and charmingly crooked." Twain's return from Darjeeling was done on the gravity cars[1] that ran on that line and, after an extensive description of the trip, Twain describes it as "the most enjoyable day I have spent in the earth."
- Twain, on riding another narrow gauge road northwest of Calcutta: "The train stopped at every village; for no purpose connected with business apparently..."
- Orwell's reference to the railways appears in *The Road to Wigan Pier* (1937), one of his numerous non-fiction defenses of socialism. It was actually quite brief: "I remember a night I spent on the train with a man in the Educational Service..." He goes on to describe the train as "jolting slowly" through the night but tells us little more about it.

---

[1] Little more than four wheels, a platform and a brake handle, the gravity cars were powered only by gravity and controlled only by the skill of the driver.

Initial Organization and Financing

The East India Company was an English joint stock company founded in the year 1600 under Queen Elizabeth I to trade in the East. Initially trade was concentrated with Mughal India and the East Indies but later it came to include a wider range of territory reaching out as far as Qing China. To protect its interests, the company ended up seizing control over large parts of the Indian subcontinent, colonizing parts of Southeast Asia, and colonizing Hong Kong after a war with the Chinese. It became synonymous with the Indian Government and, for all practical purposes, it was the government.

In the early years of the nineteenth century, the East India Company wanted railways in India for the general good of the population but also so it could move troops quickly and efficiently and so it could better exploit local resources. At the time, the textile industry was a major component of the British economy and it, in turn, was largely based on imported cotton which came mostly from the southern USA but also in smaller amounts from India. The problem was that the cotton imported from India was often damaged due to poor bullock cart transportation between the Indian cotton fields and the ports. Railroads, it was thought, would reduce this damage, improve the quality of Indian cotton as received in England, and thus benefit the English economy. The Indian Railways were thus designed and built as colonial railways: to benefit the British more than the Indians. Unlike the railroads built in the USA, there was little thought given to transcontinental transportation. In India, it was all about access to the interior.

Famine relief was another motivating factor. While famines were common in India, they tended to be local. In 1866 in Orissa, for instance, famine killed a third of the population but there were food surpluses elsewhere. The maximum range of the bullock carts was about 50 miles because beyond that distance, bullocks would consume more than they could haul. The ability to move goods longer distances would contribute greatly to famine relief.

By 1849, the Stockton & Darlington, the world's first steam-powered railway, had been in operation for fourteen years so the basic technology was well established. But nothing had happened in India despite the great demand because both the government and private capitol refused to pay for the railroads.

Then the East India Company came to terms with two private companies: the Great Indian Peninsula Railway (GIPR) and the East Indian Railway (EIR). Under their agreements, the two railways would build and operate the roads and the government would guarantee their stockholders a five per cent return on investment. The investment money came almost entirely from Britain but the risk was born by the Indian taxpayer. Naturally, since there was no incentive for them to do so, the railroads failed to earn five percent on their investment. And naturally, since the return on investment was guaranteed, the railroads invested heavily, often building their lines to the highest technical standards. In fact, the Indian Railways as a whole did not make a profit until the year 1900 when traffic finally rose to the level where the losses began to disappear. Bad harvests in 1908 and 1909 reduced earnings but in subsequent years, profitability returned, rising to 6.77% in 1912.

In return for the five percent guarantee and for its promise to provide the right-of-way, the East India Company retained the right to choose the road's routes. Further, it was given a seat on the railroad's boards, the right of veto in all proceedings, the right to purchase the roads upon expiration of the agreements (typically twenty-five years), and almost complete power over what the railroad could and would do and not do. The railways committed to carrying the mails free of charge and to the movement of military personnel and supplies at reduced rates.

The Indian rail network was built between 1850 and 1900 more or less at the same time as the US network. In India, British capitol and British engineering was used almost exclusively. Steel and equipment was also supplied from Britain and India did not begin locomotive production until 1950. Labor and low-grade manufactured items (like ties and lumber) were supplied locally. Supervision was almost exclusively British. Beginning in 1870, new construction projects were done by the state using state funds and, starting in 1880, construction was divided, done partly by the state and partly by state-aided private companies. By 1907, essentially all of the guaranteed roads had been purchased and essentially all of the main line railroads had become the property of the state although in most cases the original owners continued to operate them under new contracts with the government. By 1920 the government owned seventy-three percent of the nation's mileage. By 1922 a National Railway Control Board had been created and the work required to transfer operational authority from the private companies that had been running the roads to the board began. The roads remain state-owned today and most are now state-operated as well.

Different from the USA, the private Indian railroads never took ownership of the land they ran on; it remained the property of the government and they only received permission to build on it and use it. This, again unlike the situation in the USA, entirely relieved the Indian railroads of the need to pay property taxes.

In the early days of railroading, it was thought that the railroads would earn their way by handling freight and a limited number of relatively wealthy passengers and there was concern about how the vast numbers of the uneducated poor would react to the new technology. As service was initiated, however, it was found that the greatest users of passenger service were the poor, not the wealthy and because of their large numbers, they provided more revenue than the first class passengers. The railways made it possible for the poor to travel significant distances for the first time, looking for work, visiting relatives, attending weddings and funerals, and even taking brief and rudimentary vacations.

A fraction of the pubic did react in fear of the new technology. Some called the train an "iron demon," while others said it existed only to cheat poor Indians out of their land and possessions. Near Bombay, a rumor circulated that the locomotive was powered by children and young people who had been buried alive under the tracks. Another rumor held that by traveling fast on the train, one also sped up time itself and thus shortened one's lifespan. In another incident, the people had never before seen a locomotive and when confronted by it, they thought it evil. Fearing to get too close, they tried to drive it away by throwing stones at it. Bullock cart drivers, who were losing their jobs as the railway took over cartage, entered into a rate war with the early Great Indian Peninsula Railway (the GIPR) but they were ultimately unable to match the higher speed and lower cost of the railway and were forced to give up.

In total, the fear that the public would shun the railways turned out to be unfounded. They carried 19 million passengers in 1871, 183 million in 1901, 231 million in 1905, 630 million in 1929-30 and more than a billion in 1945-46. Freight also became heavy: 3.6 million tons in 1871; 42.6 in 1901; 116 in 1929-30; 143.6 in 1945-46. Because much of the tonnage was headed to the seaports for export, it can be seen that the railroads contributed significantly to India's position in international trade.

The first steam locomotive in India was the Thomason, a 2-2-2T tank locomotive built by E B Wilson of Hunslet, Leeds, West Yorkshire, The Thomason entered service in December 1851 working on an aqueduct construction project north of Delhi. It was a 4-foot 8½-inch gauge locomotive but was nearly the only one of that gauge ever to see service in India because Lord Dalhousie, Governor General for India, chose 5-foot 6-inches as the standard gauge for the country[2]. The Thomason ran on iron bar stock laid on longitudinal stringers (known as strap rail) and pulled 4-wheel wagons with side doors that allowed earth to be shoveled onto and off of them. It ran at about 4 mph. The Thomason ran successfully but after only a few months suffered a catastrophic boiler failure when the boiler was allowed to run dry and the resulting heat destroyed it. The locomotive was subsequently demoted to stationary use with a replacement boiler.

Dalhousie had actually wanted a 6-foot gauge but he bowed to pressure for something smaller and settled at 5-foot 6-inches which ultimately became the Indian standard. Lord Mayo, in 1870, ultimately authorized the construction of meter gauge lines. Mayo actually wanted his gauge to be 3-foot 3-inches but the nation was at the time considering adopting the metric scale. 3-foot 3-inches is only 1/3 of an inch away from a meter so the change was easy.

Power in India was split between the British Government and the East India Company until 1858. In that year, following an unsuccessful and very bloody rebellion, Queen Victoria took control back and India came under the sole control of the crown. India did not win independence from Britain until 1947.

In 1869 the government decided that railroad construction was getting too expensive so it began a program of state construction and administration along with the existing private, state-guaranteed railways. Some roads were state-built and under private management. Other roads were privately built with a lower guarantee of four percent. By 1900 there was a hodgepodge of lines with different financing (federal state, princely, private guaranteed) and management (state, private, etc.).

The government took control over freight rates, setting minimums and maximums starting in 1883.

Consolidation of at least some of the scores of railroads in India was recommended as early as 1904 but the idea did not gain much traction until 1944 and did not happen in any meaningful way until the nation was partitioned into the modern India and Pakistan in 1947. Consolidation was essentially complete by 1952.

---

[2] Lord Dalhousie was Governor General of India from 1848 to 1856 and was the person who planned (or supervised the planning of) the routes and the initial construction for the early railways. Dalhousie died in 1860.

Early Construction

The very first railway in India was constructed between 1836 and 1837 to haul laterite[3] in the Red Hills section of the city of Madras. This first railroad was powered by wind, not steam, and was closed in 1845 after less than a decade of service but while it was open, it provided a test bed for several experimental steam locomotives, most by Sir Arthur Thomas Cotton. The first of them was found to have insufficient power and too-small boilers but subsequent trials improved and finally, by August 1838, Cotton had a locomotive that could pull a train weighing some 4 tons total at a rate of 2½ miles per hour or could, without the weight of the train, accelerate to 3½ miles per hour. A month later, an enlarged locomotive reached 4½ miles per hour but then Cotton fell ill and his experiments ceased. He left India for Tasmania, apparently taking the locomotive with him. It exploded that December bringing a final end to his railroad work.

Serious, non-experimental railroad construction in India began shortly after the East India Company financing agreements were signed in 1849 and continued for decades thereafter. By 1869 there were 4,255 route miles open; by 1880, 8,996; by 1890, 16,404; by 1900, 24,752; by 1953, 34,119. The density grew from 56.3 route miles per 10,000 square miles in 1880 to 255 in 1946-47. In 1981 it was 298 route miles per 10,000 square miles and essentially 60 miles per million of population. (In the USA in 1860 there were 30,635 route miles which works out to about 98 per 10,000 square miles; in 1900 there were almost 200,000 route miles (640 per 10,000) and in 1943 there were 233,670 route miles (750 per 10,000).)

Extension of the railroads in 1870s and 1880s was driven by two considerations: famines and the second Anglo-Afghan war which was fought between 1878 and 1880.

Railways in India introduced the telegraph, created government revenue, helped with famine relief, gave market access to farmers, created employment and new classes of workers, generally boosted the economy, enabled travel, reduced commodity costs, and expanded exports and imports. Connecting the various states together encouraged national unity. Standard weights and measures

---

[3] Laterite is a soil that bears significant amounts of aluminum and iron. It typically packs easily and weathers well and is thus useful in certain low-traffic road building projects.

were introduced including standard time. On the other hand, food ended up being exported that could have been consumed in India, handcraft industries were greatly reduced by factory-made imports, money was spent on railway infrastructure that could have gone into irrigation projects for famine relief, and much tax money was spent in support of the railroads.

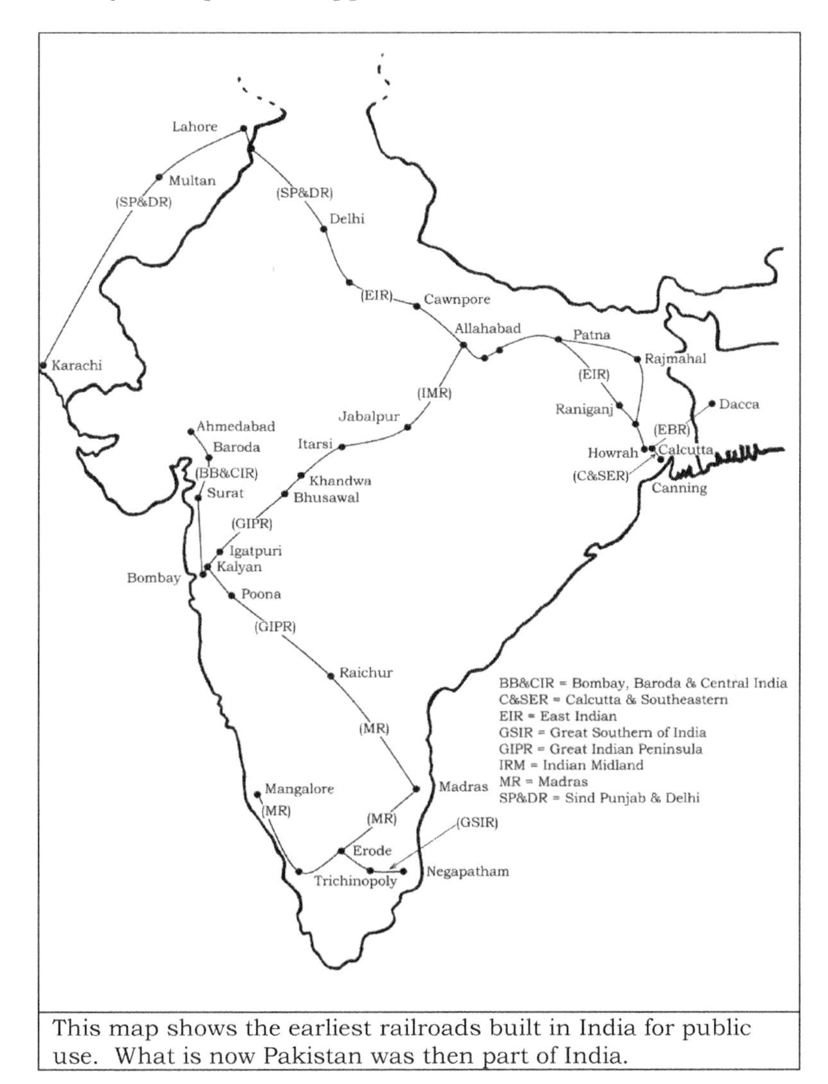

This map shows the earliest railroads built in India for public use. What is now Pakistan was then part of India.

The postal service in India didn't exist until the railroads made it possible but mail carriage on the railroads was offered from the beginning in 1854 and RPOs were in service from 1870, initially on the EIR.

Petty corruption and theft occurred as on all railroads but nothing in India approached the USA's Credit Mobilier scandal. The most significant problem was the organized theft of coal and copper, at one point amounting to one seventh of all coal purchased. Unlike railway theft in most countries, Indian pickpockets and others who preyed on the traveling public were organized into crafts, each with its own specialty, each with its own membership roll, and each with its own cadre of apprentices busily learning the trade. Some railway employees also committed thefts when opportunities presented themselves or when one could be created.

Today, the Indian Railway has dedicated police forces. The Government Railway Police are half-funded by the Indian Railway and operate under the control of the state governments. The Railway Protection Force, on the other hand, is solely an animal of the Railway Board and has armed officers on patrol. It is tasked with protecting railroad property and consigned property (shipments). In 2002 there were 54,882 members of the Railway Protection Force and active shooting situations did occur, even to the extent of a few rare old-fashioned train robberies.

One major accident in 1869 on the EIR resulted from a charging bull elephant. Other accidents over the years were caused by the usual things: misaligned switches, signal miscommunications, employee fatigue and inattention, etc. The worst came in 1981 when a cyclone blew a train into a river in eastern Bihar causing almost eight hundred deaths.

The first important railways to be built in India were the Great Indian Peninsula (GIPR; first opened in 1853), the East Indian (EIR; first opened in 1854), the Madras (MR; first opened in 1856), the Bombay, Baroda & Central India (BB&CIR; first opened in 1860), and the Sind, Punjab and Delhi (SP&DR; first opened in 1861). In 1886 the SP&DR became a major part of the North Western and in the 1947 partition of India and Pakistan, large parts of it became the Pakistan Western Railway.

Construction between 1860 and 1900 was done at a remarkably even pace averaging about 600 miles per year with variations from as little as 216 in 1883 and as much as 1426 in 1899, but without pause. The consistency was probably partly due to the distance between the work and the British decision-makers in London, partly due to the length of the Britain-India supply line, and also partly due to the limited availability of skilled labor.

Early railway construction was a boon to the brick-making industry as hundreds of millions of them were used in stations, bridges, embankments and other structures. It was also a boon to the newspaper business because it opened up markets; it is much harder to sell a day-old newspaper in a remote city than one only a few hours old.

The cost of a mile of track was about £1,700. By comparison, the same mile in England cost £31,000 and in France, £14,000. In the USA, it would have cost only £1,600 (after currency conversion) but that was largely because in the USA, tracks were laid as cheaply as possible, the idea being that they should prove themselves economically (should be profitable) before major investment was made. Elsewhere, tracks were laid to be permanent from the start.

According to one estimate, the economic savings resulting from railway construction amounted to nine percent of the Indian national income in 1900. In part because the lines were guaranteed a profit and because the government made the final decision on where they would be built, not all the lines were located in profitable regions; some met social needs. So it should not be surprising that many of the lines did not meet the 5% profitability goal and the government had to pay. Between 1879 and 1900, seventy percent of the total length of track required a subsidy in some amount.

Great Indian Peninsula Railway

The Great Indian Peninsula Railway contracted with the East India Company in 1849 and detailed surveys for the line were done between 1850 and 1851. The first train ran from Boribunder to Thana, thirty-four kilometers (about twenty-one miles), on April 16, 1853. Excepting some short and animal-powered haul lines, this railway was the first one in all of Asia and thus the 1853 inaugural train was also the first in Asia. The first train carried some four hundred passengers in fourteen cars hauled by three 2-4-0 tender locomotives: the Sultan, the Sindh, and the Sahib. The locomotives had been built by the Vulcan Foundry of Lancashire, England just the previous year.

In 1853 the land between Bombay and Thana was largely rural and agricultural. Today, during the rush hours, nine-car passenger trains packed full of riders, roar through urban sprawl at thirty second intervals. Much of this development was made possible by the railroad.

Following its 1853 opening, the GIPR was extended from Thana to Kalyan (opening on May first, 1854) and to Igatpuri at the top of the difficult Thal Ghats incline by the end of 1864. The first train to run the full length of the line to Igatpuri was pulled by the Lord Falkland, a 2-4-0 tender locomotive, also built by Vulcan. But that was not all. The GIPR was extended to Itarsi, 746 km (464 miles) from Bombay at the start of 1870. It reached Bhopal in November 1884, and Gwalior by March 1889.

The first GIPR line passed through the Kurla tunnel near Thana, the first railroad tunnel to be built in India and the first of many made necessary by the rough terrain on India's west coast.[4] From Kalyan to Kasara the line climbed by gradients of one percent and through curves of thirty chains radius (a chain is 66 feet so 30 chains is 1,980 feet or 2.9 degrees). From Kasara to Igatpuri, the grade stiffened to 2.7% and passed over one curve as tight at seventeen chains radius (1122 feet or 5.1 degrees) and the 750-foot long, 182-foot high Ehegaon viaduct.

A second line was run from Kalyan southeast to Poona over the Bhore Ghats and was opened on April 21, 1863. This line also has a 2.7% gradient, but even sharper curves (fifteen chains radius or 990 feet or 5.8 degrees), twenty-five tunnels totaling nearly twelve thousand feet in length, eight viaducts with a total length of 2,900 feet and a switchback. Routine operation featured specially-designed helper locomotives, made necessary by the curvature and grades. One of the contractors on the line, unusually, was a woman, Alice Tredwell, who took over after the early and untimely death of her husband, completing the line in May 1863.[5]

The reason why railroads first ran into and out of Bombay was the fact that Bombay was the departing point for ships bound for Great Britain. The British arrived and departed through Bombay as did mail going to and from Britain; Indians ambitious to improve their lot traveled through Bombay on their way to England and Europe. In the years shortly before World War I, trains were scheduled specifically to meet the boats arriving at and departing from the Port of Bombay.

The GIPR was acquired by the government in 1900. In 1928 the switchbacks were replaced with a new line that featured three new tunnels and electrification and in 1929 when the electrification project was finished, it covered the

---

[4] Although the GIPR tunnel was the first railroad tunnel in India, it was not the first tunnel. Remains exist of tunnels large enough for elephants to pass through that can be dated to 400-300 BC.

[5] One is reminded of Emily Warren Roebling, who took over when her husband, Washington Roebling, was disabled, and managed the completion of the Brooklyn Bridge in 1883, twenty years after Alice Tredwell.

entire line from Bombay to Igatpuri via the Thal Ghat and from Bombay to Poona via the Bhore Ghat.

East Indian Railway

Calcutta was the national capitol of India until 1912 so it was natural that the East Indian Railway was planned to run from Calcutta to Lahore via a string of major cities that included Patna, Moghal Sarai, Mirzapur, Allahabad, Cawnpore, Agra, Delhi and Ferozepur. In addition, there were coal fields in Raniganj. The P&O Steamship Company wanted access to that coal and also to the cotton fields in the central part of India.

The line actually began at the city of Howrah rather than Calcutta because the Hooghly River that runs between Howrah and Calcutta was seventeen hundred feet wide and the company, in a situation reminiscent of the Pennsylvania Railroad's entrance to New York City, wanted to avoid building a major bridge.[6] In the end, the Hooghly was not crossed by a high level bridge for almost forty years and the city of Calcutta remained cut off from its train station in Howrah for all that time.

The East Indian Railway was officially organized in May 1845; surveying began in July and was completed in April 1846. A contract was signed with the East India Company on August 17, 1849 specifying that the East India Company (the government) would provide the land and select the route while the East Indian Railway would perform the actual construction, provide rolling stock, and operate the line. The agreement further specified that the railroad would carry postal bags and post office workers free of charge and would take troops and other government officers at reduced fares. It also provided that the railway would become the property of the government in ninety-nine years or sooner if the parties involved agreed on an earlier date. Construction was started in 1851 with the section from Howrah to the city of Hooghly, 37.47 km (23.28 miles) complete on August 15, 1854.

The initial construction would have allowed an opening of part of the line before the GIPR's opening and that would have made the EIR the first railroad in India. But the EIR's official opening was delayed until February 3, 1855 after a consignment of carriages was lost in the sinking of the *HMS Goodwin* in the Hooghly River and after much delay caused by the shipment of the line's first locomotives to Australia by mistake. Although the carriages could be replaced

[6] The Hudson, however, is more than twice as wide as the Hooghly.

by local craftsmen, the locomotives could not. Further, there were delays caused by border disputes and by citizens who objected when their land and the buildings on it were taken by the East India Company for the railroad's use without compensation. Complicating the situation, all British material for the new railroad had to be shipped around Cape of Good Hope as the Suez Canal did not then exist.

Because of the topography and climate, these two lines (the GIPR and the EIR) were as difficult to build as any anywhere else in the world. In the 1859-1860 rainy season, a cholera epidemic killed as many as ten percent of the workers weekly and lasted through October and November of that year. No exact accounting was made but the death toll likely totaled between four and ten thousand.

The completed line proved to be worth the work it had taken to build it. During its first sixteen weeks of operation, no less than 109,000 passengers were carried on the newly-born EIR. This exceeded expectations and encouraged further construction. The line was finished as far as Raniganj later in 1855 and carried an average of nearly 12,000 passengers a week which the British directors considered "most satisfactory." In its first year of operation, 1855, the line carried a total of 617,000 passengers and by the end of that year, was carrying coal at the rate of 100,000 tons per annum. The 1857 Santhal Rebellion (see page 37) delayed further construction but did only minor damage to the work that had been completed. The line between Allahabad and Cawnpore was completed in 1858 before Allahabad was connected to the line from Calcutta but the gap was soon filled.

Early in 1859, the Chief Engineer and his assistant, who were both British, were attacked and murdered by a party of rebels. The rebels and their ringleader were subsequently caught, tried, and hanged. By the end of 1859 there were nineteen passenger and thirty freight locomotives running, eight passenger and twenty freight locomotives under construction or repair, 228 passenger coaches, and 848 freight cars. During 1859 the road carried 1,388,000 passengers and hauled 299,000 tons of freight.

The first train from Calcutta to Rajmahal ran on July 4, 1860 and the road was opened the full distance on the following October 15th. At that point the company had 249 miles in service in the state of Bengal and 126 miles in the North-West provinces. Later in 1860, 87 more miles were opened between Cawnpore and Etawah.

After the coal mines were reached at Raniganj, the government, which was the route-determining body, changed its mind on the railroad's route and a new line was started more closely following the Ganges River from Burdwan north to Rajmahal and then from there to Patna. The new line was significantly longer than the original proposal and the delay in constructing it is said to have cost the British much during the Rebellion because it took three weeks to move troops as far as Benares when it could have taken as little as a day. What's more, once the line reached Rajmahal, the Ganges had changed its course and at least some of the original benefit had disappeared. On the other hand, the relocated line passed through a number of large and densely-populated areas and thus provided service and earned revenue that the original alignment would have missed.

Work continued despite delays caused by this indecision and others concerning the line's route. It was not until April 1864 that the entire line was open between Calcutta and Delhi and even then the bridges over the Jumna River at Allahabad and Delhi remained incomplete. The Allahabad Bridge, which was opened on August 15, 1865, had been under construction for almost eight years. The bridge at Delhi opened in 1866 and was the last of the great bridges on the line. The distance from Calcutta to Delhi was then 1,020 miles which made the EIR, at that moment, the longest railroad line in the world.

At first, the EIR was poorly equipped, lacking sufficient passenger and freight cars and lacking adequate terminal facilities in many places. Despite this, a chord line connecting Raniganj and Patna was soon put under construction as a way of shortening the route by almost a hundred miles and also as a way of avoiding the double-tracking of the line through Rajmahal. Difficulties with a variety of contractors caused delay but the "chord line" was finally opened in 1871.

As the chord was being built, a problem arose: the laborers began to claim illness and to refuse to work as the grade approached the small town of Talgaria (known as Jharkhand today). Investigation revealed that the site chosen for the Talgaria station was the site of a suti, a sacred spot where a widowed woman had caused herself to be burned alive on her husband's funeral pyre. Ultimately the tracks were diverted a few meters to miss the hole in the ground that marked the suti and an iron plate was lowered over it to protect the people's religious sentiments.

In 1866, for the first time, the railroad earned more than the government-guaranteed five percent, enabling a dividend and relieving the government of its obligation. More than four million passengers were carried and over eight hundred thousand tons of freight were handled that year. The service provided, however, was less than excellent due to the huge volume of business and the fact that the railroad had not been designed to handle that much. Arrangements were made for the purchase of an additional two hundred fifteen locomotives and similar quantities of rolling stock and plans were made for double-tracking the line where bottlenecks restricted flow.

There was a cotton boom in 1866 but a depression followed it in 1867. Both had their effect on the railway. As a result, some double-tracking projects were delayed, third class fares were reduced, and the line's organization was improved by the elimination of some redundant workers.

In 1867 a voluntary retirement plan named the "Provident Institution" was instituted for both European and non-European employees. Terms and conditions varied over the years but basically the plan was funded by employee contributions and by company contributions from its annual surplus (when there was an annual surplus). The collected funds were then invested and the proceeds used to pay retirement wages. Like today's Social Security, while the plan worked, it was only of assistance in retirement and did not pay enough to fully support a retired worker.

In 1888 the EIR opened a school for the sons of its European employees at Jherapani, a place in the hills with a reasonable summer climate. (Subsidies were provided for native staff sons' educations at other schools.) In 1897, land nearby was purchased and a similar school for girls was opened. Later that year, the North Western, which also operated schools for the children of its employees, closed its schools and began to send its children to the EIR schools. Two years later the government assumed ownership of the schools but left management and control in the hands of the railroad.

In 1867 a branch from Allahabad to Jabalpur was opened and, with the completion of the Indian Midland's Itarsi-Jabalpur line in 1870, the long-sought Bombay-Calcutta transcontinental trunk route became a reality. According to Lord Mayo, Viceroy, in a speech delivered on the occasion of the formal opening, £22 million had been invested in the Indian railway system to that point, four thousand route miles were open to traffic, a thousand more were under construction, and nine hundred more were about to be started.

In 1872 and again in 1902 tornados blew over mixed trains near Rampore Hat station a bit more than a hundred miles north of Calcutta. The trains were both stationary at the time. In the 1902 incident, only twenty-eight of the three hundred passengers were injured or killed.

Several railroads were built that were effectively branches of the EIR, but were built to the meter-gauge to save costs: The Rajputana State Railway between Muttra and Hathras (afterward extended to Agra and Cawnpore and later leased to the broad gauge Bombay, Baroda & Central India Railroad); the Delhi-Umballa-Kalka Railway; a 2-foot 6-inch gauge railway between Kalka and Simla known as the Kalka-Simla Railway (now part of the North Western system); and the South Behar Railway from Luckieserai Junction to Gya. All of these lines subsequently suffered from transshipment costs at their connection with the broad-gauge EIR.

The rains failed in 1873 and as a consequence, there was famine in the Bengal region at the end of that year and well into the next one. The EIR proved its worth by moving 750,000 tons of grain into the area. To accomplish this, the railroad needed thirty additional locomotives and forty-six new personnel to operate them. Another famine followed in 1876, this time in the Madras and Bombay areas, resulting in more heavy grain traffic and this time also resulting in a severe car shortage due to the greater distance the grain was being sent.

When built, the EIR installed its own telegraph lines on one side of the tracks and subsequently the government installed a second line on the other side. In 1877 these two independent systems were merged under government ownership and maintenance, effecting a significant cost reduction.

Coal traffic had been significant but had been largely limited to railway and local use, there being little export market at the time. Significant coal deposits were owned and worked by the railroad but the government objected to that, saying that it was inappropriate given the government's profit guarantee of five percent. An argument was advanced based on the Aesop fable of the golden goose and apparently it gained some traction because the mines remained with the railroad and remained open.

In 1881 the opening of the meter-gauge Rajputana-Malwa Government Railway on the west side of India brought about a rate war between that road and the BB&CIR on one hand and the EIR on the other. In effect, the city of Bombay was vying for trade that had flowed through Calcutta to central India but which could now flow through Bombay at reduced shipping cost from and to Britain. After some hesitation, the government decided that the railway managements should be allowed to establish their own rates in competition with each other within government-established minimum and maximum values. While Bombay had a superior harbor and a shorter sail to England, it had little access to coal for its railroad and many mountains to deal with. Thus costs were high. Calcutta and the EIR, on the other hand, had a lesser harbor and a longer sail, but much lower operating costs because it did not have to import coal or fight grades.

On January 1, 1880, the government purchased the East Indian Railway but retained the corporate structure and its personnel to manage and operate it. At the time, the railway was 1,504 miles long and it constituted sixteen percent of the total of all Indian railways, which were 9,148 miles in length. There was one mail train and one through passenger train in each direction each day. The passenger train took fifty-three hours to cover the 954 miles at an average speed of eighteen miles per hour; the mail train ran faster, averaging a bit more than twenty-two miles per hour. Third class fares were experimentally reduced by one-sixth and the people responded with increased patronage to the point where the total receipts grew almost ten percent.

Branch lines were built to reach newly-discovered coal fields at Jherriah and Toposi with construction done from 1892 to 1894. Upon completion, the Bengal-Nagpur Railway was given permission to enter the field but it was never serious competition to the EIR because its route to Calcutta was significantly longer than the EIR's.

Revenue from coal haulage in 1891 was a little more than 6.3 million Rupees; in 1896, 9.7 million; and in 1901, 18 million. By 1906, coal movements constituted more than half of the freight handled by the EIR.

By that time, domestic coal use was only nominal with the vast majority going to export (the British India Steamship Company being a large customer). A shortage of rail cars and terminal facilities constrained the coal export trade but even then in Calcutta it amounted to 137,000 tons in 1891, 574,000 in 1896, 1,995,000 in 1901 and 2,767,000 in 1905.

The Jubilee Bridge across the Hooghly River at Calcutta was opened on February 16, 1885 in the fiftieth, or jubilee, year of the reign of Queen Victoria. Construction had begun in 1882 and was completed in 1887. The bridge served until it was decommissioned in 2016.

The Jubilee Bridge made possible a connection to the newly constructed Kidderpore Docks over the Eastern Bengal Railway. Initially intended for grain and seed export, the docks attracted some coal traffic but were never popular with the grain shippers, who preferred the docks in Howrah. During 1897, 2,040,000 tons crossed the Jubilee Bridge and in 1901 that number rose to 3,613,000, 83% of which was coal.

In 1889 the "fast train" covered the distance from Howrah to Delhi, 954 miles, in 37½ hours at an average speed of a little less than twenty-six miles per hour. There was no significant signaling system, and the trains were fitted with only manual brakes. By 1906, a block system had been installed throughout the entire length of the line and vacuum brakes had been installed on all cars and locomotives. Train times were reduced to 28½ hours (thirty-three miles per hour). Equipment shortages were largely eliminated by 1900-1902 except for freight cars which were chronically short during high traffic periods. A twenty-four percent increase in freight car inventory between 1900 and 1905 only slightly exceeded a twenty-one percent growth in traffic over the same period.

There was an outbreak of plague starting in the spring of 1898 and much of Calcutta abandoned the city making it almost impossible for the EIR to unload freight cars there.[7]

EIR shops were established at Jamalpur. (Distinct from Jabalpur, Jamalpur is a hundred miles or so east of Patna.) The town had no access to raw materials or to coal and all had to be brought in, but it was in an area where for centuries iron had been made and worked and one in which there was a source of skilled labor. First established in the early 1860s as an engine-changing point, by the early years of the 20th century, the shops covered a hundred acres (twenty under roof) and employed more than nine thousand. Fully self-contained and self-sufficient, it was capable of building new locomotives from raw materials but also did locomotive maintenance and car building and it manufactured cast-iron ties (sleepers) and signaling and interlocking gear. The local supply of water was quite limited and, at times, it was necessary to run water trains from the shores of the Ganges, some six miles away. Electric power was first provided to the shops in 1901.

Competition in 1906 included boats on the river, the Bengal-Nagpur Railway which paralleled the Jubbulpore branch, the Bengal & North-Western that ran along the Ganges but on the other side from the EIR, the Southern Punjab and the North-Western Railways.

All in all, the EIR was a highly successful enterprise. Around the year 1900, third class passenger traffic amounted to ninety-five percent of all passengers

---

[7] Plague is a bacterial infection that is transmitted primarily by fleas. Antibiotics developed in the 20th century now control the disease although about 600 cases still appear worldwide each year.

and eighty percent of all passenger revenue. India was a nation of poor people and the fares were such that a laborer could travel twenty-one miles on a day's earnings. In the UK, that person could travel forty miles and in the USA, sixty miles. Fares in India, therefore, were high considering the nation's wealth. In 1905 twenty-two million third class passengers were carried on the EIR.

Madras Railway

The third railroad to start operation was the Madras, built in southern India. Its first section, sixty-three miles between the cities of Madras and Arcot (almost due west of Madras) opened in July 1856.

An earlier Madras Railway had been chartered in 1845 but ran into difficulties and was dissolved in 1847 before doing anything significant. The successful one was chartered in July 1852 and construction began in 1853. The initial goal was a line across the Indian peninsula from Madras on the east coast to Beypore on the west, some 820 miles.

During the 1850s and 1860s, construction costs averaged £18,000 per mile and, on top of that, operating costs exceeded revenues making it necessary for the government to pay even more to meet the five percent guarantee. A mile of construction in the 1860s required the transport of six hundred tons of material from Britain. According to *Trains Magazine*, Grenville Dodge once estimated that the building of a mile of track on the US transcontinental railroad required forty carloads of material.

Early lines were built to 5-foot 6-inch gauge which is, coincidentally, the same gauge as San Francisco's BART subway system (although it is about the only thing that BART and the Indian railways have in common). As of 1967 the Madras system remained about half 5-foot 6-inch gauge and half (or a little less) meter gauge with a few miles of still smaller gauges sprinkled around here and there. Rather than having regional gauges (as in the South and in Colorado in the US), in India the longest mainlines were 5-foot 6-inch and the local feeder lines were either meter-gauge or smaller.

Actually there is controversy over whether the division in gauges was a good thing for India or not. It is true that a gauge break is much less important when passenger service is concerned because passengers load and unload themselves without cost. It is also true that the narrow gauge railways in India carried only a small amount of freight (about fifteen percent of all ton-miles) and thus the cost of gauge transfers was small but some have argued that the reason why the amount of freight handled was small is the cost; had the lines been built to broad gauge like the rest of India, the economy would have developed differently and those lines that handled little freight would have handled much more.

Taking the narrow gauge idea to its extreme, there was a period between 1902 and 1927 when several attempts at monorail operation were made; none were notably successful.

The British government wasn't unaware of the problems that a break in gauge would cause. The importance of rapid troop transport argued against the construction of narrow gauges but it ultimately lost out to the counter-argument that if narrow gauges could not be built, the economics of the situation would prevent any railroad at all from being built in many portions of the country. A narrow gauge road, it was said, is better than none at all.

Madras Railway construction began in 1856 and 136 miles of line were completed by 1860 running from Madras to Arcot and beyond. By 1871 the Madras ran 374 miles from Madras to Raichur where it met the GIPR. Several branches were added and then, in 1907, the entire line was purchased by the government. In 1908, the Madras was combined with the Great Southern to make up the Madras & Southern Mahratta Railway.

Bombay, Baroda & Central India Railway

The Bombay, Baroda and Central India Railway was built as a broad gauge line north from Surat into Gujarat to Ahmadabad then built south from Surat along the coast to Bombay. It was initially a government guaranteed line with the guarantee set at five percent. By 1860 there were thirty-five miles in operation and 219 under construction and, by 1870, construction was essentially complete. Unusually, a branch line to Wadhwan, built in 1872, was converted to meter gauge in 1902; most gauge conversions were in the opposite direction.

The Rajputana State Railway opened in 1874 running from Bandikui north to Delhi and east to Agra. The line continued on to Ajmer and Ahmadabad. The Holkar State Railway built north from Khanwa, ultimately reaching Ajmer and merger with the Rajputana in 1882 to form the Rajputana Malwa Railway. In 1885 the Rajputana Malwa was leased to the broad gauge Bombay, Baroda & Central India Railroad and thus the BB&CIR came to have a substantial meter-gauge component. Ultimately an aggregation of twelve separate railways, the entire system was purchased by the State in 1906 although it continued to be operated by the former owners. In 1942 the government took over operation and in 1951 the BB&CIR became part of the new Western Railway zone.

The BB&CIR was a substantial railway rostering, over the years, nearly a thousand locomotives. As with other railroads of India, the earliest locomotives were 2-4-0 and 0-6-0 but they were joined after World War I by groups of 4-6-0, 4-4-0 and 4-6-4 locomotives and, in the late 1920s by 4-6-2s and 2-8-2s. The BB&CIR named a good many of its locomotives with the names, as elsewhere in India, being drawn largely from British aristocracy. There was, however, a group of 4-6-2 Pacifics named after Indian cities: City of Delhi, City of Baroda, City of Indore, etc.

In 1928 the BB&CIR purchased three twin-unit articulated rail cars from the Sentinel Wagon Works of Shrewsbury. All three units served up to World War II but were taken out of service by 1944.

North Western Railway

The North Western Railway resulted from the 1870 merger of the Sind Railway, the Punjab Railway, and the Delhi Railway, all of which were governed by the same board of directors as the East Indian Railway. After the merger, the combined roads, known as the Sind, Punjab and Deli Railway, ran north from Karachi and south-westward and eastward from Lahore toward Multan and Delhi for a total of 364 miles. They gave India access to the strategically sensitive border with Afghanistan so, following the merger, the line was almost immediately purchased by the government. The Punjab Northern State Railway, the Indus Valley State Railway, and the Kandahar State Railway were later built and, when merged into the SP&DR in 1886, the result was the North Western Railway.

Terrain crossed by the NWR varied from heat and humidity on the coast at Karachi to even greater heat in the Sind desert and to mountain cold and snow in the north. Rainfall varied from five inches per year to five inches per hour. Grades on the line were up to four percent, bridgework totaled ninety-two miles and the road included the longest tunnels in India.

Surveying for the Sind Railway was first authorized in December 1853 but the man chosen to do the survey, a Lieutenant Chapman, was drowned in a boating accident on his way to begin the work and the result was a two-year delay. Following the survey, the first dirt was turned in 1858 and construction began. Short pieces of the line were opened in 1859 but they were used almost exclusively for construction and it was not until 1861 when first hundred miles of the line between Karachi and Kotri was opened to regular commercial traffic.

To get to Delhi from Karachi in those days required taking the railroad to Kotri, which was on the Indus River, and then getting on a boat to travel up the river 570 miles to Multan. From Multan, the traveler would then take the Punjab Railway another 254 mules to Amritsar via Lahore and the Delhi Railway from Amritsar on to Delhi, another 300 miles. This avoided the dangerous tidal delta of the Indus River and also its upper shallows but the trip still took five weeks on the water and days more on the railroads. The need for a faster route was obvious.

As built, the Sind Railway was single-tracked with passing tracks at five intermediate stations and with a short 2¼ mile stretch of double track at the Karachi end. It was built to the then-standard Indian broad gauge of 5-foot 6-inch. The Indus Valley State Railway, which paralleled the river, was first imagined as meter-gauge but was actually built to the broad gauge, saving much work and many delays in transit. The broad gauge choice, however, was not made to control transit costs and delays but was made largely due to the high winds that often roared through the Indus Valley. The additional stability the broad gauge theoretically offered was seen as critical. Unfortunately, initial clearance standards were tight in bridges and tunnels and past station platforms so cars and locomotives were smaller than optimum and carrying capacity was similarly reduced.

While the earth was relatively flat making Sind Railway construction easier than in the mountains, sudden storms and high rates of runoff made finding footings for the railroad difficult. Thirty-two bridges were required and the last one was not finished until 1861. Girderwork was standardized and iron bridges were built in England, shipped to India, and assembled on site by local workers. The initial rail used was sixty-five pound and double-headed, intended to be turned over after wearing down but it was found that the rails moved in their seats and that wear to the bottom side was comparable to that on top. Block signals were used from the beginning under the control of telegraphed orders. The entire line was fenced so locomotives were not provided with cow-catchers. The first were four 2-4-0 tender locomotives made by Kitson & Co of Leeds in 1858. Following were a group of seven 2-2-2 "singles" and thirteen 0-6-0 freight locomotives. All were coal-burning.

The Punjab Railway extended from Amritsar to Multan and the Delhi Railway from Amritsar to Delhi where connection was made with the East Indian Railway to Calcutta and with the GIPR and the BB&CIR to Bombay. Built without a single significant bridge, the Punjab Railway was intended to replace the steam boats that ran between Multan and Lahore over the difficult and treacherous Indus River. Built as 5-foot 6-inch broad gauge, it occupied the high land between the Ravi and Sutlej Rivers and had a straight 114 miles long and a maximum grade of one in six hundred. It was built as a single track line but land was set aside to allow for future double-tracking.

Delivery of the first locomotive to the Punjab required that it be brought by boat from Karachi and then dragged up the hill from the river to the tracks. One report says that the haulage required 102 bullocks with two elephants pushing at the rear. Regular service began on May 1, 1862 with two trains daily (one on Sundays) from Lahore to Amritsar. After much delay, the line south to Multan was opened in April 1865. The first trains did not run at night but night running was introduced in the summer of 1866. Early locomotives on the Punjab included ten 2-2-2s, five 0-6-0s and twenty 2-4-0s, the last having 60-inch drivers.

The Delhi Railway was opened in 1865. Unlike the Punjab, it was heavily bridged, crossing the Beas, Sutlej and Jumna Rivers. The bridges were initially mounted on poorly-built piers and in just a matter of a few years, they had to be replaced.

As was true elsewhere in the world, the early construction years were punctuated with instances of corruption, mismanagement and malfeasance. The SP&DR was especially hard-hit in this regard resulting in a series of official investigations, a number of early and forced retirements and resignations, and even some criminal proceedings. In the United States, the Credit Mobilier and Erie Railroad scandals caused the government to back away and regulate at arms-length; in India, the scandals made the government lean in closer and ultimately contributed to the government's decision to take over the railways.

The merged railway was called the North Western because it was in the northwestern corner of India when it was built even though, today, it is almost all in Pakistan. Broad gauge for the most part, it was double-tracked in the south and the east and, through acquisitions, included small segments of 2-foot 6-inch gauge and significant amounts of meter gauge, particularly at its south end. An extensive network of broad gauge branch lines and secondary mains covers the countryside north of Samasata.

With partition, the railway was split in two with the Pakistani portion becoming the Pakistan Western Railway and the Indian portion becoming the Northern

Railway. At the time of partition, the NWR was the longest railway on the Indian sub-continent.

The Indus River runs north to south more or less along the modern borders with Pakistan and Iran. During World War II it was seen as a natural line of defense in the event of a German invasion so all the railroad bridges across the Indus were fitted with explosives to make it easy to deny them to the enemy. As it turned out, there was no invasion and thus none of the bridges had to be blown.

The Punjab Northern State Railway was state financed and state-owned. Built initially to meter gauge, it was widened to the 5-foot 6-inch gauge in 1878. The government's goal was to provide access to the frontier so the line ran north from Lahore a hundred miles to Jhelum, opening in September 1876. River crossings were important on this line and were initially made with floating pontoon bridges which, in times of flood, had to be withdrawn so they were soon replaced with iron spans of the deck truss and through truss types. Because the rivers became so wide when flooded, the bridgeworks were literally miles long. Unfortunately, there was essentially no bottom to the alluvial soil so piers could not be founded on rock.

The Chenab River Bridge was equipped with a road surface so it could be used by ordinary traffic between trains. Due to the length of the bridge (1¾ miles), two places were built where traffic traveling in opposite directions could pass. Eighty-three piers were required and up to a hundred thousand bricks were laid daily during the three working seasons it took to construct the bridge. Adequate labor was unavailable locally so large numbers of workers had to be imported. Then, in the 1873-74 flood season, the river changed course and some parts of the bridge had to be redesigned and rebuilt. But finally, in December 1875, the first meter gauge train passed over it. Formal opening was done in January 1876 by the Prince of Wales (later King Edward VII) and the bridge was named the Alexandra Bridge after his consort.

But the Alexandra Bridge was no more complete than the decision was made to convert the lines of the Punjab Northern to the 5-foot 6-inch gauge. The roadway was removed, saving enough weight so that the original iron work could handle at least some broad gauge trains in safety. Further strengthening was completed by November 1891 and the diversion of river water for irrigation purposes reduced flow to the point that the original number of sixty-four spans could be reduced to seventeen. Another round of strengthening, competed in 1926-27, replaced the original iron with steel Pratt trusses.

The sixteen-span Empress Bridge across the Sutlej and Beas Rivers was built between 1873 and 1878 on the line between Kotri and Multan which had originally been serviced by boats on the Indus River. It completed the rail connection from the port of Karachi to Lahore with the exception of the crossing of the Indus River in Upper Sind between the towns of Sukkur and Rohri which continued to be done by ferry until the opening of the Lansdowne Bridge in 1889.

Throughout the second half of the nineteenth century, India greatly feared a possible invasion by Russia through Afghanistan so in 1876 the decision was made to construct a railway to Quettah in Baluchistan. The Kandahar State Railway, as built, ran from the Indus Valley State Railway near Sukkur toward Kandahar but never crossed the border and ended at Chaman, some 323 miles away. War did break out that year (1878) but the Scindia and Indus Valley Railways were still isolated since the bridges at Attock and Sukkur had not been completed. The countryside crossed is largely flat desert plain with sparse vegetation for the first forty miles but then nothing. Some locomotives carried two tenders to assure a water supply. Because the line was built in a hurry, supplies came from many sources and thus were not standardized. There was flat-bottom and double-headed rail and four distinctly different kinds of mountings which made organization at the end-of-track difficult. Some six hundred men were employed simply to unload materials from trains, load it onto carts, deliver it to the place where it was needed and unload it.

In lieu of completion of the railroad to Kandahar, the Indian government built a supply depot in Chaman and stocked it with enough material to build the last sixty-seven miles should an emergency arise.

The possibility of a Russian invasion was apparently real. Between 1884 and 1888, Russian General Annenkov used Russian troops along with local labor to build the Transcaspian Railway from Krasnovodsk on the Caspian Sea in Turkmenistan 1,150 miles to Tashkent in Uzbekistan. The bridge over the Amu-Darya River had been a challenge; the structure finally completed was so flimsy that the rules required every train to follow a man on foot across it, thus assuring modest speeds. Although the potential was there, the line was never extended into Afghanistan and thus it never really threatened India. But, of course, no one knew that in 1888.

Prior to World War II, all bridge work had been built in England, disassembled, moved to India, and reassembled on site. Following the war, however, the Nari Bridge at Sibi desperately needed strengthening but none of the bridge-making firms had time on their schedules to do the work. Ultimately the Government decided that the new girders should be built in the railway's own bridge workshops in Jhelum. It was the first time an Indian firm had fabricated girders out of new steel.

The extension of the Punjab Northern State Railway from Peshawar to the Afghan border ran through an area that was subject to extreme flooding, river levels of as much as seventy and even one hundred feet above slack water being recorded at various times. When the Afghan war broke out in 1879, work was started immediately and was completed to either side of the river by the end of 1880. The first serious proposal for a rail line included a tunnel below the river at a place called Attock. Digging was begun and serious progress was made but waterproofing it and making it useable turned out to be beyond the abilities of the technology of the day so the tunnel was never completed. A bridge was built instead.

Opened in 1883, the bridge at Attock consisted of five spans, three of 257 feet and two of 312 feet, the longest in India. The girders were among the first mild steel construction in India. The last span was closed up on March 3, 1883 and, at the end of that month, an earthquake shook the bridge so violently that it was displaced an inch at the tops of the trestles but the bridge survived, passed its final tests, and entered service. Forty years later, in 1926, it was found to be in badly decayed condition and was rebuilt and double-tracked with new piers between the old ones. In 1929, as the new work was nearing completion, it was found that the Shuyok Glacier 600 miles up the Indus from Attock had made an advance, blocked a valley and created a huge temporary lake fourteen miles long and between one and three miles wide. The glacier failed in August 1929 and the resulting flood rose to within inches of the record depth. The new bridge held but it was almost certain that the old one would not have survived.

The bridge across the Indus at Khushalgarh was built to replace a rope cableway. Over the years tracks had been laid to each end of the cableway and it had been improved so a single 4-wheel freight car could be lifted and hauled across the river without unloading but it was a slow, cumbersome and expensive process. When, in April 1903, a cable anchorage failed, dropping an entire car of grain into the river, it became obvious that a bridge was needed. A two-span cantilever bridge was designed using, of all things, an aerial ropeway to lift the steel into position. It was competed and opened for traffic in 1907.

The railway reached Peshawar in 1883. In 1901 it was extended twelve miles toward the Khyber Pass to Jamrud. Khyber Pass was even more difficult than Bolan Pass or Hurnai Pass, at least insofar as the local tribes and local opposition to construction were concerned. When work began to extend the railroad another thirty miles through the pass to Landi Kotal, a chain of fortified posts was built overlooking the line and all stations on the line were built as forts with the ticket windows designed to do double duty as machine gun loopholes in the event of need. The extension was completed in 1925; the line required thirty-four tunnels, ninety-two bridges and culverts, and four switchbacks.

It is said that the Sultan Khel was opposed to the railway and was ready to fight to prevent its construction until someone pointed out to him that the trains would move slowly over the steep and winding track and thus would be easy to pillage. Khel, apparently, was won over by this argument. He allowed the building of the road in hopes of future plunder from it. The person pointing out the slow speed was one of the engineers involved in the construction of the railway.

Two years after the opening of the Attock bridge, in May 1889, the Lansdowne Bridge across the Indus between Sukkur and Rohri was opened, making possible through train service between Lahore and Karachi. At the time of its construction, it was the longest rigid girder bridge in the world, but that record was eclipsed by the Forth Bridge in Scotland which opened in March 1890. The Lansdowne Bridge is actually two bridges: one from Sukkur reaches halfway across the river to the island of Bukkur; the other from that island to Rohri. The Sukkur end of the bridge turned out to be relatively routine since the channel there had a solid bottom suited for the construction of piers; the Rohri end, however, has no such bottom, making piers impossible. After many designs and much consideration, a pair of anchored cantilevers was built, each 310 feet long and with a center suspended span of 200 feet. The bridge, as were most on the Indian railway system, was designed and built in Britain, then disassembled, shipped, and reassembled over the river. The size of it all made necessary the assembly of girders weighing 86 tons apiece in the air, 180 feet above the ground. And all this work was done under the Indian summer sun with heat soaring to unbelievable temperatures. It was originally intended that the center span be assembled on shore, floated into position, and lifted up to close the bridge but river conditions made this impossible so an entirely separate temporary staging structure had to be built to allow the span to be assembled at its actual point of use.

The Lansdowne Bridge was in the desert and not subject much to corrosion but constantly subjected to extreme temperature variations. As locomotives and trains got larger and heavier, it was strengthened in 1910 and again in 1934 when the dead weight of the roadway was removed, forcing road traffic to detour five miles to cross the river. As the years passed, consideration was given to replacing it but nothing happened and World War II intervened. Following partition, Pakistan chose to erect the Ayub arch a few hundred feet from the Lansdown Bridge. It was the first in the world to have a railway deck slung on coiled wire rope suspenders. Work began in 1960 and the bridge was opened to traffic in the spring of 1962. The Lansdowne Bridge was then converted for sole use by light vehicles, pedestrians and animals.

As originally built, the Indus Valley State Railway had run up the west bank of the Indus River from Kotri to Sucur but that line missed the important city of Hyderabad which lay on the east bank. The bridge at Kotri was opened in 1900, allowing the railroad to construct a double-track line all the way from Karachi to Samisata on the east bank passing through both Hyderabad and Rohri. The new line was thirty-eight miles shorter than the old one and traveled through much less challenging country with few hills and curves. The bridge was paved, allowing use by the public between trains, and two light pathways were cantilevered from the sides to accommodate foot traffic. Between 1931 and 1933, the bridge was heavily reinforced to allow it to carry much heavier trains and the cantilevered pathways were strengthened and widened to twelve feet for general use by animals, carts and motor vehicles.

In an attempt to reach the Afghan frontier, the Sind Peshin State Railway was built northwest from Sibi with the first short section completed in January 1880 but Sibi marked the boundary between the desert and the mountains so the challenges were very different. Shortly after starting work in what was potentially enemy country, the troops that protected the workers were withdrawn to meet an emergency elsewhere and construction thus came to a stop. Activity by the Russians restarted the project in 1883 but, since the government did not want it known that work was underway, the project was titled the Harnai Road Improvement Scheme and neither rails nor rolling stock were purchased. That policy eventually changed, the road was renamed the Sind Peshin State Railway, and in March 1887 trains began to run through Bolan Pass to Quetta, about halfway to the border. Plans called for the line to continue on through Bostan and then to penetrate the Khwaja Amran mountains with India's longest railway tunnel. The line was to terminate in the town of Chaman, extending to within a few hundred feet of the border.

The Bolan Pass, along with the Khyber Pass, was the main invasion route from Afghanistan into India. Over five thousand years of recorded history, it is believed that twenty-six invasions have taken place, almost all of them successful. It was, therefore, natural for India to want to defend the route.

Sibi is 433 feet above sea level with an average shade temperature in the summer of 96 degrees Fahrenheit and with occasional spikes in the 120-degree range. The summit is at Kachh Kotal, 6,533 feet above sea level. Oil was discovered at a place called Khattan and it was used as fuel for the engines driving the tunnel-boring machinery when the Khojak tunnel was under construction. Then, eighty-two miles from Sibi, coal was found and, with the technology of the 1880s, it was far more valuable than the oil so the oil fields were shut down.

Local tribes were opposed to the railway and attacked the workers, killing several in raids reminiscent of Native American raids in the USA. More serious, however, was malaria which was common where the heat of the desert met the wet of the mountains. Thousands of workers died. And according to one source, even today the area is lawless and travelers are on occasion held to ransom.

The Khojak tunnel was designed with a hump in its center to promote drainage. The hump, however, meant that the locomotives had to work hard as they passed through and thus they generated large amounts of smoke and gas. Knowing this would happen, the tunnel designers specified a number of ventilation shafts but the local banditry soon found that rocks could be dropped down those shafts onto the tracks and, with a little luck, directly onto a train. Ultimately the shafts had to be bricked up and the line turned to the use of gas masks to protect the locomotive crews.

Bolan Pass is a narrow slit in the mountains that allows the line to be built at a lower altitude than if it were to go over the top but with the disadvantage that the pass sometimes fills with runoff after storms. The railroad, therefore, had to be constructed above the floor of the pass and in some very inaccessible places. At one point, a construction road was needed where it seemed that none could be built but the problem was solved by driving iron bars into the rock face and using them to support a narrow plank road.

Acknowledging the difficulties of Bolan Pass, an alternative route from Sibi to Quetta through the Chappar Rift and the Dozan Gorge, was begun in April 1885 and completed in 1895. It had its own difficulties including much tunneling and bridging and, remarkably, was built with a section of meter-gauge track tucked into the center of the broad gauge line. With curves of two hundred foot radius and grades of one in twenty-three (4.3%), the meter-gauge segment was originally planned as temporary. The Abt rack-and-pinion system[8] was used to

---

[8] The Abt rack-and-pinion system is based on a Swiss patent. It uses a double rack down the center of the track with the teeth offset. They are engaged by

allow trains to climb through the area. In 1888 work began on the broad-gauging of the line with reduced curvature but unchanged grades. But in 1889 a flood washed away the bridges and in 1890 even bigger floods completely removed all traces of the railroad. The solution was to build yet another railroad on another alignment, this one being higher in the Dozan Gorge and thus, hopefully, out of the reach of the floods. As it turned out, that third line was not out of the reach of earthquakes and in 1931 it was hit by a major one. There were no fatalities but luck played a major role in that the quake hit during the daytime when people were mostly outdoors and at a time when the mail train was halted in the station of Machh. Oddly, a bridge just above Machh was shortened by twelve inches in the quake; the piers and bridgework remained undamaged and only the anchorages needed to be corrected before the newly shortened bridge could be put back in service.

At a place called Mudgorge, there is a glen about three miles long that is filled with dried gypsum mud some seventeen hundred feet deep. When the weather is dry, the surface of the mud is solid but after rain it becomes a morass and the soil swells and heaves. At one point a thousand feet of the railway simply disappeared. The first workable solution turned out to be a cut and cover tunnel through the mess combined with a drainage system that drew water from the tunnel across the gorge to the other side.

And Mudgorge was only one of the problems. The Nari Gorge and the Nari River had to be crossed six times. The Gundakinduf Defile, about eight miles long, required two tunnels and four bridges. And the Chappar Rift required a horseshoe curve, a series of tunnels and the Louise Margaret Bridge, all to keep within the ruling gradient. An order was placed with Alfred Nobel for a hundred tons of dynamite.

Cholera and malaria were unrelenting problems particularly around Hurnai. Very high wages had to be paid to attract a continuing flow of new workers. Through the summer of 1886 the workforce had to be renewed every two months to replace those who died of disease and accident.

The road sees such extremes of climate that it was built in sections, working the upper levels in the summer and the lower ones in the winter.

---

two driven axles on the locomotive, each carrying two pinion gears so there are always two teeth engaged as the train moves.

On July 11, 1942 an unprecedented flood roared through the Chappar Rift, washing away the railroad and ending rail service forever. The rails and many of the bridges were removed and the steel used in the war effort.

The Kandahar State Railway thus ran from Sukkur to Sibi and two lines, the Sind Peshin and the Muskaf Bolan, from Sibi to Bostan. The goal had been to reach Kandahar so the next step was the construction of the Chaman Extension Railway, sixty-eight miles long, from Bostan to Chaman on the border with Afganistan. The line would rise from an elevation of 5,193 feet at Bostan to 6,394 and then drop to its terminus at 4,304. In heavily mountainous territory, it featured six tunnels, one of which was the Khojak. At 12,870 feet, the Khojak was the longest railway tunnel in India at the time of its construction and was also the first one drilled through water-bearing strata that required heavy timber bracing. A group of sixty-five Welsh minters was specially recruited for the job as they had experience on the Severn tunnel between England and Wales and other, smaller tunnels in Wales. Work on the tunnel began in April 1888 and the first 5-foot 6-inch gauge train steamed through it in September 1891. Construction involved several interesting features including temporary inclined planes to lift railroad cars up the steepest hills. And oil-fired engines were used to power the air compressors, winding gear and other equipment; oil for these engines was brought in on camel-back. The final ruling grade worked out to two-and-a-half percent although in sections it is much less. 2-8-0 steam locomotives struggled with it, a daily fruit train passing through before 1947.

The road was optimistically named the Kandahar Railway and it was generally headed in the direction of Kandahar, Afghanistan but it never got that far. Ultimately reaching Chaman on the Afghan border, it came to a halt.

1942 was a year of exceptional floods following four quiet years where there had been essentially none. On July 22 the river topped its banks and many of the levees (or bunds as they are called in India) creating a huge gap one-and-a-half miles across through which water was pouring at the rate of 150,000 cubic feet per second. The last train arrived in Sukkur just before 10:00 PM and the road was out of service for three months thereafter.

That same flood also cut the line between Lahore and Delhi, although in only one place. As it was wartime and traffic on the line was seen as critical, a bridge was designed and built to span the new riverbed. It was in service nine days after the line had been cut.

One of the most famous of all Asian railroads is the Khyber Railway which runs through the Khyber Pass on its way between India and Kabul, Afghanistan. Not built until 1926, the railroad replaced two roads and an aerial ropeway with a single broad-gauge track. Work began on the railway in 1920 and, when complete, it included four switchbacks, thirty-four tunnels and ninety-two bridges and culverts. Although the line has a ruling gradient of three percent, it is broad gauge, eliminating the need for transshipment of goods and has only modest curvature with generous clearances.

Only one railway line extended beyond the border of India (now Pakistan). The Nushki Extension Railway (part of the North Western) ran along the Afghan border into Iran, terminating at the city of Zahidan. It was built during World War I to replace a route that previously could only be traveled by camel but was seen as essential to the national defense. Two-hundred-forty-two miles long and broad-gauge, it went through a region that was uninhabited and essentially without vegetation, without rain and with only dry rivers. Moving sand dunes filled some of the area and the railroad discovered that when a dune covered the tracks, it was easier and simpler to build a new line behind the dune and wait for it to move on than to attempt to dig away the thousands of tons of sand involved. There is little traffic on the line and in 1932 much of it was taken up but was replaced again when World War II entered the picture. In 1948, as part of the Pakistan Western Railway, service on the line was increased from two trains weekly to three.

The North Western was built as a broad-gauge 5-foot 6-inch line but it came to include eight narrow-gauge lines totaling 769 route miles of track. Of those eight lines, seven were thirty inch gauge and one was twenty-four. As were many such lines all over the world, the choice of narrow gauge was universally made as a temporary expedient to be replaced by the broad gauge when time and finances allowed. Some were actually converted while others were closed without ever seeing broad gauge track but most continued through their lives as narrow gauge in a broad gauge world.

Construction Labor

In India, railway construction was subject to three levels of control: in Britain, in India at the capitol of Calcutta, and at the job site. The Chief Engineer at the local job site had reporting to him several junior engineers, each of which had reporting to him assistant engineers, one for each ten to forty mile section of track. The assistant engineers were the people who stood on the line, directed thc work, and madc the final, detailed decisions. Beneath them were overseers (often ex- of the British Indian Army) and beneath them the workmen.

A "navvy" was a migrant unskilled or semi-skilled laborer who worked on infrastructure projects like railways, canals, roads, and ports. When a project was done, the navvy would move on to another project in another location rather than look for different work. The term was an abbreviation of "navigator." Navvys were generally paid about two or three times as much as an agricultural laborer, justified by the fact that they led a nomadic life style without the comforts and securities of a fixed home.

Most early construction was done using third-party contractors. Unlike some of the contractors who built the railroads in the USA, the Indian ones were independent of the railroad's owners. Some were among the first large-scale contractors in the world, being among the first to have investments in equipment and in workforces who would travel from jobsite to jobsite with the work. Previous to the late 1860s, contractors had been people who hired locally and who required their workers to provide their own tools and equipment. Other Indian railway building was done by smaller contractors who were supervised by engineers working either for the railway company or the state. Still other construction was done by railway workforces under the management of the railways.

Construction employment averaged some two hundred thousand workers between 1859 and 1900.

The Indian caste system presented problems as the members of one caste often would not work beside the members of another. Cholera and malaria presented health issues and the obtaining of supplies was a problem. Termites attacked most of the wood used for ties. In addition, there were engineering problems with difficult river crossings. What in 1850 and 1860 was experimental, became mostly routine by 1900.

In 1855, almost half (forty-nine percent) of the workers employed were women; fourteen percent were children; thirty-seven percent were men. In India, the work of earth movement fell to the women since it was done by carrying earth in baskets. The truly heavy work involving strenuous lifting was done by men. By contrast, in Britain women never worked as construction labor and their use in that role in the USA was rare.

Mechanization was slow. Riveting, as an example, was entirely manual until 1887 when a hydraulic riveter was introduced on the Dufferin Bridge across the Ganges at Benares. Even then, it was only used some of the time and manual riveting continued to be the more common method.

A properly-organized and well-run plate-laying (track-laying) gang could put down a half-mile of new line a day.

The "Tommy-shop" or "company store" where workers received supplies and paid for them by having them charged against future wages was commonly used in India as it was in some places in the USA. In both instances, prices charged were often high.

Construction was complicated, among other things, by the Santhal Rebellion of 1855-56 and other disruptions in the mid- and upper-Ganges valleys in 1857-1858. The rebellion, known as the War of Independence or the Great Mutiny (depending on which side you were on) began north of Delhi in May 1857 while the EIR was in the middle of surveying (in some places) and construction (in other places). The Santhal people had been forced from their land by the colonial rulers and rebelled against their eviction. In January 1856 the British government moved against the Santhals and brutally put the rebellion down. In 1857, a more general "Indian Rebellion of 1857" occurred and it lasted through most of 1858. Work was halted, some stations and bridges were destroyed, and many Europeans were forced to flee and/or defend themselves.

There is an obvious analogy between the Santhals and the American Indians in the USA. Both were indigenous ethnic groups which had lived on the land for thousands of years before the Europeans showed up. In both cases, they were forcibly removed from land and in both cases, the result was violence. Like at least some of the American Indians, the Santhals had bows and arrows and axes but their opponents (the Sepoys, infantrymen serving in the British Army) had firearms so the ultimate outcome was never in questions.

Troops were brought in by steamship to help quell the mutiny, one of the first large troop movements by that method, emphasizing the value of steam power in military matters and further encouraging the construction of the Indian railways. In those days, as especially in India, when an Army traveled by rail, it didn't necessarily arrive sooner than if it had marched, but it did arrive in better condition and more able to fight.

At one point during the revolution, steam locomotives were loaded on barges and their wheels were used to drive paddlewheels to move the boats. The barges were used both for troop and supply transport and, after the war was over, for the movement of material to the railroad which was still under construction.

Defenses on the western entrance to the tunnel at Kojak Pass in what is now the province of Baluchistan, Pakistan made it look almost like a castle. This photo was taken in 1895 by William Henry Jackson and was saved in the collection of the Library of Congress. [Library of Congress]

The completed sections of the EIR also proved very useful in troop movement. As with the US Civil War, the railroad was damaged but was able to recover relatively quickly after the end of hostilities. One of the more lasting effects on the railway was the design of tunnel portals, bridge approaches, station buildings and other facilities with an eye to defend-ability. Castle-like crenellations, narrow archer's windows, and other gothic embellishments appeared here and there.

The disturbances added steam to the railway construction efforts because they emphasized the value of fast troop movements. Railroad construction after the rebellion was more controlled by strategic considerations and less by commercial ones. The disturbances also resulted in a considerable increase in labor cost and wage rates.

In 1859 the workers on the GIPR rioted when the contractors, who were months in arrears with wage payments, began to make those payments at half the promised rate. Europeans were stoned and one was killed but police were brought in, legislation was rapidly passed to diffuse the situation, and eventually everyone went back to work. By 1905, Indian Railways employed 437,535 of which 6,320 (one-and-a-half percent) were "Europeans" (almost all British) and 8,565 (two percent) were Anglo-Indians (people with one British and one Indian parent). The Europeans overwhelmingly held the highest-ranking positions and the Anglo-Indians a middle stratum. The 422,650 remaining employees were Indians who held the lower ranking positions.

To some degree the British had difficulty adapting to the Indian climate of heat, humidity and various tropical diseases. It was found that the Anglo-Indians, having been born on the Indian peninsula, were somewhat better adapted and, in addition, were cheaper to employ. Not only did they work for lower wages, they also required no travel between England and India. Anglo-Indians thus began to replace the British in railway jobs, particularly those in the middle stratum.

Railroads required a cultural change for the indigenous Indian employees. The work required promptness and diligence that had not previously been a part of life. The concept of central management and the bureaucracy that goes with it was new and irritating. And the people began to discover that the railroads drove increasing specialization on their villages, crops and manufactures. The railroads made it possible for localities to import goods that had been previously unavailable and this meant that there was economic advantage to concentrating one's efforts on producing what one could grow or make most efficiently. That increased efficiency provided enough earnings to pay for the imports and kept the cycle going.

Historically, poverty in India arose from the disincentives inherent in the caste system, from the lack of a universal language, from the climate, from prevalent diseases including cholera, malaria, smallpox typhoid, pneumonia and others, from a lack of education, and from the drain of resources to England. While the nation's huge population did not contribute to wealth, it also did not contribute directly to poverty.

The unionization of the Indian Railways and the development of collective bargaining more or less paralleled similar developments in other countries. The first union appeared in 1897 and the first strikes occurred on the EIR and Eastern Bengal in 1906. Prior to World War I, strikes were rare and unusual but the war provided significant profits which led to growth both on the railways and in the unions after the war. During 1921 and 1922 there were forty-eight strikes lasting from a day or two to three months. In 1924, the All India Railwaymen's Federation brought together more than a dozen individual unions with a total membership of over two hundred thousand. The unions achieved much in terms of worker rights, pay and working conditions but suffered along with all other organizations during the depression.

The railways created a workforce that did not fear industry or technology and one that respected precision and punctuality. In 1865 the railways employed 34,000 workers; in 1895 the number was up to 273,000; in the late 1920s it was 790,000; and by 1946-47 employment reached 1,047,000.

The great depression, as measured by railway freight tonnage in India, had only a small impact in the early 1930s but the lost ground was made up well before World War II began as wartime profits brought an end to deferred maintenance. By the time of World War II, essentially all the Indian railroads had been taken under government control and ownership. Indians started moving into management positions in the mid-1920s but the official language of the railroads was English and that slowed promotions. By 1947, management was almost entirely Indian.

By 1970, India had the largest railroad network in the free world that operated under a single management (globally second only to the USSR) and new lines continued to be constructed. By 1981 the system consisted of 2,654 miles of narrow gauge, 15,763 miles of meter gauge, and 19,361 miles of 5-foot 6-inch gauge. In 2020, the Indian Railway system provided employment to more than 1.4 million people and at least one source claims that it was the largest private employer in the world. In modern times, many railroad employees got housing, medical care, education, recreation and more along with their wages.

Technology

The Government Steam Train ran on the Grand Trunk Road in 1872 and was, for a time, very successful.

[P S A Berridge, *Couplings to the Khyber: The Story of the North Western Railway*]

While this might sound like something that happened in Canada, it wasn't. Improved roads were a new concept in India in the early part of the nineteenth century. The Grand Trunk Road was an ordinary, graded highway that had been built in India by Lord William Bentinck between 1828 and 1835, was opened between Calcutta and Delhi in 1839, and was extended to Peshawar, a total of fifteen hundred miles, in the late 1850s. Designed for use by bullock carts at a top speed of two miles per hour, the Grand Trunk Road was well graded, smoothly surfaced, tree-lined throughout its length and featured stopping places every ten or fifteen miles.

The Government Steam Train was a steam-powered tractor that pulled a string of four-wheel and two-wheel carts along the road at higher speeds than the bullocks. Ultimately four tractors were built under the auspices of the Indian Post Office and hauled loads of up to forty tons routinely between Rawalpindi and Attock, a bit more than fifty miles. They were among the first to use differentials on their driven axles and among the first to be fitted with rubber tires for traction. The death of Lord Mayo (Richard Southwell Bourke, Viceroy of India), who had been an ardent supporter of the Government Steam Train, brought them into full competition with the railways and after a few years of declining service, their primary use changed to one of local travel.

The first steam engine had been brought into India in 1820 by missionaries at Serampore (on the north side of Calcutta) so the fundamental idea of mechanical power wasn't new. Other stationary steam engines were installed and run in Bombay in 1923 and Calcutta in 1828. The one in Bombay helped power a cannonball-making factory while the one in Calcutta pumped water.

Most of the early Indian railroads were built as single track but the East Indian Railway main line from Calcutta to Delhi was double tracked from the beginning. The initial policy was, however, that all earth-work and masonry should be done to accommodate double tracking even though only a single track was to be laid.

The loading gauge on the Indian broad gauge lines allowed only 9 foot 6 inch car width which does not take full advantage of the 5-foot 6-inch track. In much of the USA, the gauge allows 10 foot 8 inch width on 4 foot 8½ inch track. Unfortunately, in India much of the double track was laid to allow only this 9 foot 6 inch width and that limitation kept the railway's ability to haul wider rolling stock at a minimum until finally, in 1945, a program of separation of the double-track lines was begun, moving them to a 15 foot 6 inch center-to-center distance. The work was completed in 1951.

The first rails were sixty-five pound wrought iron double-headed on stone sleepers. Flat bottomed rails and wood ties gained popularity and rail weight rose to eighty pound with forty and fifty pound rail on the narrow gauges.

Sleepers (or ties) were a problem due to rot and insects and their average life was only seven years. In some areas telephone poles were uprooted by elephants and had to be protected with rings of iron spikes.

The great bridges were all iron because iron bridge spans could be longer than masonry ones and longer spans meant fewer piers and less supporting structure. Because essentially all work was done by hand, the erection of a pier was a massive undertaking and was not to be attempted unless truly necessary. In the early years there were many bridge failures although the number of failures declined as the builders gained experience. The BB&CIR bridge across the Narbada River in western India suffered flood damage twice during its construction, was opened to traffic in 1861, was seriously damaged in 1864, 1865 and 1867 and was nearly destroyed in 1868. Then, in 1871, major bridges across the Jumna, Sutlej and Beas Rivers were seriously damaged by flooding and the Beas river damage was made vastly more serious when a passenger train was dropped into the river below.

Masonry was frequently used as a low-tech building method but it wasn't always successful. By the late 1960s, over two thousand GIPR bridges, buildings and other masonry structures had failed. The collapse of the Mhow-ki-Mullee Viaduct in 1867 was a spectacular example. A track walker noticed movement under his feet. He ran from the viaduct and reached safety at its end before it collapsed. Freight trains from both directions managed to stop before plunging into the chasm and no one was hurt but the road was out of service for a long time. The viaduct was eventually rebuilt and, decades later, was replaced with an earthen embankment.

Technology came to the Indian Railways slowly, but it did come. Human and animal labor was used in earthmoving well into the 1960s. When the Bezwada

Bridge was built in the 1890s, bullocks were used to dredge out the foundation wells. On the other hand, electricity appeared as early as 1911, used to light the construction of the Hardinge Bridge over the Padma River so work could continue at night. Lessons learned as the nation's bridges were built were soon transmitted outward and India thus paid for the knowledge it had imported by contributing to the overall level of worldwide engineering skill.

After the First World War, good times returned. The railroads continued to expand, growing from a total of 35,129 route miles in 1920 to 39,678 in 1929, an increase of thirteen percent.

Electric traction had been discussed as far back as 1904 but work did not begin until the technology gained broad popularity in the 1920s. Design actually began in 1922 based primarily on French technology and skills, and it wasn't until 1925 that the electrification of the Harbor Branch of the GIPR between Bombay and Kurla was opened for a distance of nine and a half miles. Sections of the BB&CIR and the Madras were also electrified with the work stating in 1928 and completed in 1931. Taking advantage of the favorable worldwide economy of the late 1920s, additional track was laid and improvements were made in bridges, yards, shops, and stations as part of the electrification project. By 1929 electrification was completed to Kalyan, a total of thirty-three miles. Between 1929 and 1930 the mountainous main lines between Kalyan and Igatpuri (fifty-two miles) and those between Kalyan and Poona (eighty-six miles) were electrified using fifteen hundred volt DC traction with sixteen substations installed along the route. This greatly increased the capacity of and speed of the trains. In 1931, the meter gauge track between Madras Beach and Tambaram and in 1936 a section of the BB&CIR between Borivli and Virar were electrified.

Bombay is built on a group of what was once seven islands protruding from the mainland out into the Indian Ocean. The islands limit development possibilities in some ways much as New York City (also an island city) has been limited. In both cases, substantial suburbanization and heavy-duty commuter railroads have been the solutions to almost unbelievable overcrowding. And in both cases, traffic on the commuter railroads was heavy enough to easily justify electrification.

Bombay suburban lines were fully electrified by 1936; a Madras suburban line in 1930. These electrifications and later work in Calcutta (1957), made possible heavy-rail commuter lines and those lines, in turn, made possible the growth of the cities. In 2018, Bombay (Mumbai since 1995) was the world's seventh largest city with a population of 20 million.

The new commuter lines, being independent of the other railroads, were not limited to existing standards so broader track spacing was defined and cars purchased that were twelve feet in width and sixty-eight feet long. The third class cars each seated ninety-six.

Electrification proceeded beyond Igatpuri toward Bhusaval on a 191-mile double-track broad gauge mainline in the 1960s. Construction began in Calcutta in 1973 and ten miles from Dum Dum to Tollygunge became operational in 1995. That line now runs eight-car trains on three minute intervals during rush hour. The Delhi Metro has been in service since 2004 running Korean-built electric multiple-unit cars.

All electrification was done at fifteen hundred volts DC until the three thousand volt DC electrification of the Howrah-Burdwan section of the Eastern Railway entered service at the end of 1957. More or less at the same time, however, based on experience on the French Railways, the decision was made to convert to twenty-five thousand volt AC power. The first twenty-five thousand volt AC section opened for service was Raj Kharswan–Dongoaposi on the South Eastern Railway in 1960. The first twenty-five thousand volt AC electric multiple-unit cars began suburban Kolkata service in September 1962. The Howrah–Burdwan section of the Eastern Railway and the Madras Beach–Tambaram section of the Southern Railway were converted to twenty-five thousand volt AC by 1968 and the Mumbai suburban rail network in 1996–97. Today the entire electrified mainline rail network in India uses twenty-five thousand volt AC, with DC traction used only for metros and trams.

Indian Railways announced on 31 March 2017 that the country's entire rail network would be electrified by 2022, primarily to save on imported fuel costs.

State Ownership, Merger and the Partition

The guarantee plan under which the early railroads were built was needed to encourage capitalists to invest in the roads but it turned out to be expensive for the government because, with the guarantee, there was no incentive for the roads to build or operate economically. The government had included buy-out options in the railroads contracts and, starting in 1879 with the East Indian Railway, those options began to come due and the government began to take over. Although it bought the EIR, the government did not immediately assume operating responsibility but instead contracted with the existing operators to continue operations. The GIPR, the BB&CIR and the Madras were subsequently not purchased but were given new contracts with a revised and less generous guarantee. The Eastern Bengal Railway, the Sindh, Punjab & Delhi Railway, the Oudh & Rohilkhand Railway, and the South Indian Railway, however, were purchased and were subsequently operated by the government while others continued under private operation by the companies that had previously owned them. The concept of government ownership and private operation was essentially unique to India.

In the 1880s, several famines hit India and the government realized that it needed to build more railroads quickly. The money required was hard to find, however, and the government ended up going back to the private capitalists under a revised version of the old guarantee system. This resulted in the construction of the meter gauge Indian Midland and Southern Mahratta and the broad gauge Bengal-Nagpur Railways.

In 1900 there were ninety-six railway lines serving the Indian pubic, operated by thirty-three separate companies.[9] With every railroad managed and owned under a different contract with the government, the situation soon became incredibly complex. In 1905 a Railway Board was implemented within the government to devote its full time to the operation and management of the railways. After several adjustments, notably those resulting from the Acworth Committee investigation of 1921, that board still exists and still operates the railways. It consists of a chairperson and eleven members and directors who work at the highest level of India's civil service aided by a vast cadre of assistants extending down to the level of the clerks and typists. The board reports

---

[9] While impressive, this number pales when compared to the approximately twelve hundred US railways listed in the 1900 Official Guides.

to the Parliament of India through the Ministry of Railways headed by the Railway Minister of India, since 2017 a man named Piyush Goyal. The Minister is a political appointee while the others are civil servants.

The Indian people argued and fought for independence throughout the period of British colonialism. The desire for independence and nationhood spilled over into a desire for nationalization of the country's largest industry: the railroads. Mahatma Gandhi, who was important to the struggle, was a frequent traveler and was very familiar with the railroads. In 1893, long before he became famous, Gandhi was thrown out of a first class carriage and that experience, it is said, motivated him to reject British imperialism and begin his fight for independence. In the years before World War I, Gandhi traveled frequently by third class coach and quickly became a critic of the dirt, the uncomfortable cars, the crowding and the impoliteness of the railway workers. According to Gandhi, the third class passenger paid about a fifth of what the first class passenger paid, but received far less than a fifth of the services in exchange.

Less well known is the fact that one of several attempts to assassinate Gandhi involved the railway. Gandhi was traveling on a train that came at speed upon a blockade made of rubbish laid across the tracks. Gandhi's train was the only one scheduled for that time and the fact that he would be on it was well–known so the assumption is that assassins hoped to create an accident and an opportunity to murder the controversial leader. The train's driver, however, was alert and was able to bring the train to a stop in time to avoid the accident and thus the murder. Symbolically, when Gandhi died in 1948, his ashes were carried to Allahabad in a third-class railway carriage mirroring how he had lived his life.

During World War I the railroads, like railroads everywhere, were overwhelmed with traffic. A government take-over, as done in the USA, wasn't possible because the government already had control. But new rules and regulations reduced passenger traffic to let freight flow more easily, fares were increased and pilgrimages prohibited. Not only was the traffic intense during the war, under British control much railway manufacturing was diverted to the manufacture of armaments and other war materials and still more material in the form of rails, bridges, locomotives and cars, was taken from the country for war use elsewhere, mostly in the Middle East. The result, at the end of the war, was a badly worn out railroad system in India and a much increased public demand for local control over the railroads.

In 1921 a committee headed by Sir William Acworth recommended that all Indian Railways be managed in India, that all management contracts with British firms be terminated, and that management should be transitioned to the State.

The GIPR and EIR systems were brought into the state railway system in 1925 (both had been state owned but privately operated), BB&CIR and the Assam-Bengal Railway in 1942, and almost complete nationalization was completed by 1944 when the Bengal-Nagpur Railway was taken over. The railways were made independent of the government by establishing a separate budget for them and removing them from the general government budget. This gave the Railway Board control over its finances and thus control over the destiny of the railways.

Standard time zones were adopted in the USA in 1883 but were somewhat later in India. The railroads (and the pubic) dealt with local time zones in Calcutta until 1948 and in Bombay until 1955. Local clocks were synchronized daily via telegraph from a central timekeeping office at railway headquarters. Although India is nearly thirty degrees wide on the globe and thus large enough to encompass two fifteen-degree time zones, the nation uses a single time zone for simplicity and is five-and-a-half hours ahead of Greenwich, England.

World War II affected India much as had World War I with huge demands made for production and support of the British in many ways but differed in that in World War II, the Japanese became combatants. They invaded Malaysia and, in effect, stood at India's door. This brought British troops to India to defend the empire, but it also contributed to the near exhaustion of both the soldiers and the railroads. By the time the war was over, it was obvious that British rule over India was approaching an end.

American troops also fought in India, taking control over several railroads, rebuilding broken-down equipment, tightening schedules, and importing both locomotives and cars to add capacity. Sidings were lengthened to speed the flow of traffic, two new ferry terminals were built, train lengths were doubled and train speeds were nearly doubled. American jeeps were given flanged wheels and used as locomotives. The meter gauge Assam-Bengal Railway was especially affected.

Prior to 1947, the Indian Railways had been almost uniformly profitable with operating ratios around seventy percent even in the depression and below fifty percent many of the years between 1853 and 1946. Between 1880 and 1910 both freight and passenger rates actually came down; these were growth years and the railroads were able to take advantage of economies of scale; the reduced rates increased traffic to fill the new lines and still left significant funds for profit.

For political reasons, the British chose to walk away from India in February 1947, leaving behind two new countries: a shrunken Hindu India and Moslem Pakistan. This resulted in massive violence and wholesale slaughter as Hindus, Moslems and Sikhs battled for land and for control. As had been the case with the railroads in the US Civil War, the railroads of India found themselves in the middle of it all.

Pakistan was initially divided into two pieces including a primarily Bengali-speaking East Pakistan. In 1971 in a separate blood-soaked independence movement, East Pakistan became Bangladesh.

It is estimated that a half million people died at the time of Partition and twelve million more became refugees as the Indian Moslems struggled to reach Pakistan and the Pakistani Hindus to reach India. Pakistan and India subsequently fought two wars and conflict continues even today in the Kashmir area which is largely Moslem but remains part of India. Between August 27 and November 6, 1947, 673 refugee trains were run transporting 2,300,000 people. By the end of October the worst of the violence was over but while it was going on, trains were attacked, crews refused to work for fear of the violence, much last-minute re-routing was done to avoid trouble spots, and some five thousand officials and their families ultimately had to be flown across the border.

Partition of India and Pakistan tore the North Western into two railroads, the Pakistan Western and the Northern Railway of India, with the former ending up larger by a significant fraction. By 1958 a quarter of the train-mileage on the Pakistan Western was diesel-powered with diesels coming from Alco, General Motors, General Electric and Alstom. Electrification was planned on the Pakistan Western using fifty-cycle single-phase system for the lines between Lahore and Rawalpindi (178 miles) and between Lahore and Khanewal (153 miles). Dams planned on the Jhelum River at Mangla and on the Indus River at Tarbela would help reduce the instance of flooding and thus the cost of annually reconstructing flood-prone portions of the line.

The lines that made up the Pakistan Western had originally been designed for the Indian Military and thus were of much less value to Pakistan. Route mileage was reduced in both Pakistan and, later, in Bangladesh as highways were built and cars, trucks and motorcycles became more common.

There were other problems. Over the years, some skills had effectively become Moslem and others Hindu. Partition meant that both railways developed significant skill shortages as people left their jobs and moved to meet the demands of partition. It also meant the replacement of the British senior railway officials with Indians and, for all reasonable purposes starting in 1947, the railways were entirely run by Indian nationals.

The North Western Railway, which had been operating 6,881 route miles in colonial India, was reduced to 1,855 miles after Partition. Similarly, the Assam-Bengal Railway was reduced from 3,555 route miles to 1,942 within India. Much railway equipment was cut off from its normal repair shops by the new international boundary.

Nationalization created a single, impossibly huge railway that was simply too big and too complex to be efficient. Between 1951 and 1952 the gigantic Indian Railway was divided into six smaller railways which the Indians called zones. The intent was that each zone should be geographically as compact as possible, that each should be large enough to support a full staff and its own workshops, and that each should be operated in effect as an independent railroad.

The original six zones were made up as follows:

- The Southern Zone from the Madras & Southern Mahratta Railway, the South Indian Railway, and the Mysore State Railway
- The Central Zone from the Great Indian Peninsula Railway, the Nizam's State Railway, and the Scindia & Dholpur Railway
- The Western Zone from the Bombay, Baroda & Central India Railway, the Saurashtra Railway, the Jaipur State Railway, the Rajasthan Railway, and the Cutch Railway
- The Northern Zone from the Jodhpur Railway, the Bikaner Railway, the Eastern Punjab Railway and part of the East Indian Railway
- The Eastern Zone from the Bengal-Nagpur Railway and part of the East Indian Railway
- The North Eastern Zone from the Oudh & Tirhut Railway and the Assam Railway

The zone structure was complete by April, 1952 but almost immediately began to disintegrate. In August 1955 a new South Eastern Zone was split off from the Eastern Zone and in 1958 the Northeast Frontier Railway was separated from the North Eastern Zone.

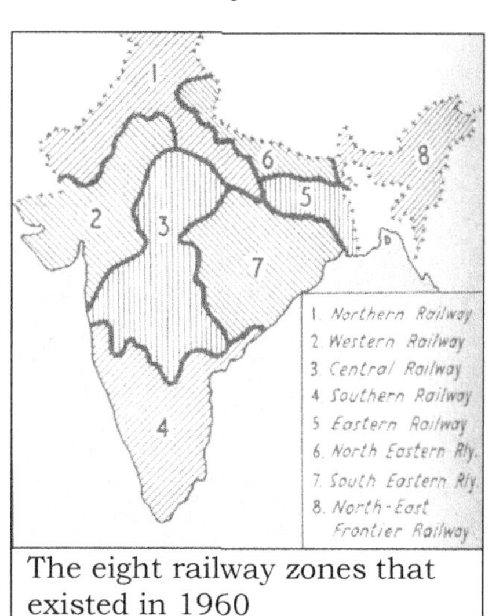

The eight railway zones that existed in 1960

Subsequent political pressures created yet another zone in 1966. Then, in 1992, seven additional zones were created, making the total sixteen. Adding zones, of course, reduced their size and presumably allowed zone management to focus more closely on the issues of the areas and peoples it served. To this extent, more zones might have been a good thing. It is also true, however, that having more zones meant having more administrative staff and, in some cases, more workshops and more service facilities and this might have increased cost.

Today there are eighteen zones:

Zone	Headquarters
Central Railway	Mumbai
East Central Railway	Hajipur
East Coast Railway	Bhubaneswar
Eastern Railway	Fairley Place, Calcutta
Metro Railway	Park Street, Calcutta
North Central Railway	Allahabad
North Eastern Railway	Gorakhpur
North Western Railway	Jaipur
Northeast Frontier Railway	Guwahati
Northern Railway	Delhi
South Central Railway	Secunderabad
South Coast Railway	Visakhapatnam
South East Central Railway	Bilaspur
South Eastern Railway	Garden Reach, Calcutta
South Western Railway	Hubballi
Southern Railway	Chennai Central
West Central Railway	Jabalpur
Western Railway	Mumbai (Churchgate)

The zones are headed by general managers who report to the Railway Board and are further subdivided into sixty-eight operating divisions, headed by divisional railway managers.

Nationalization also brought about a rationalized system of freight tariffs which were implemented in 1948, improved in 1958, and further changed in the 1990s. A protocol for shipper's complaints about rates was established using a body called the Railway Claims Tribunal. That tribunal, always chaired by a retired Federal Judge, made only binding, un-appealable decisions, a structure with interesting ramifications.

Partition left Kashmir part of India (although disputed by Pakistan) but without rail contact with its mother nation except by going through Pakistan. Thus construction of the twenty-seven mile Mukerian-Pathankot line began in 1949 and was completed in 1952. Subsequent work extended the line fifty miles to Jammu and beyond that to Srinagar. In the Northeast a similar situation left Assam without rail connection to the rest of India so construction began on the hundred-forty-three mile long Assam Rail Link in 1948. Built through malaria jungles, mountainous terrain, and an annual rainfall exceeding two hundred fifty inches, the line was completed in just two years.

The Indian Railways, like many systems all over the world, worked after World War II to promote tourism with regional offices in a number of major cities around the world. Some railways operated their own hotels and many accommodated traveling parties with special onboard accommodations.

The 1960s were a time of retraction and shrinkage on the railways of the USA but a time of growth for those in India due to ongoing development in the country and greatly increased trade.

In the 1963 fiscal year:

- The Central Railway consisted of 7,144 km of single track and 1,680 km of double and quadruple track. There were 931 stations. 402 million passengers were carried along with 40 million tons of freight. The line had 1,538 steam locomotives and 116 diesel; 2,549 passenger cars, 376 EMU coaches, 51,000 freight cars, and a staff of 207,240 people.
- The Eastern Railway consisted of 2,453 km of single track line and 1,596 km of multi-track line. There were 579 stations. 295 million passengers were carried along with 64 million tons of freight. The line had 1,502 steam locomotives and 156 diesels and electrics, 2,989 passenger cars and 64,000 freight cars. As part of a mechanization program, a ballast tamper was purchased and placed in service. A new diesel locomotive shed was completed and placed in service in Patratu.
- The North-East Frontier Railway completed several new lines and installed new centralized traffic control. The road consisted of 3,022 km of single and 22 km of double track with 464 stations. Meter gauge dieselization began in 1962 with sixty units in service by the end of 1963.
- The Northern Railway completed significant improvements including double tracking in Utter Pradesh, a new bridge over the Robertsganj and the intro-

duction of a new meter-gauge diesel rail car for suburban Delhi service. 189 million passengers and 43.5 million tons of freight were carried.

- The Southern Railway operated 9,986 km of single and multiple track lines with 1,344 stations. 252 million passengers were carried along with 23 million tons of freight. The line had 1,755 steam locomotives and 4 electrics, 3,838 passenger cars, 30 EMU cars, and 36,700 freight cars. It employed 168,593 people.
- The South Eastern Railway made up only ten-and-a-half percent of the route-miles of the Indian Railway System, but moved over a quarter of the total freight. Major capital work was under way including new bridges and conversion of lines from two- to three-track. Coach yards were built or remodeled and a new line was built to serve the port of Haldia. The first Indian-built AC electric locomotive was placed in service. That year, the road operated 10,249 km of single- and multiple-track lines with 625 stations. 93.9 million passengers were carried along with 56.5 million tons of freight. The line had 1,097 steam locomotives, 79 diesels and 69 electrics.
- The Western Railway continued to expand electrification and double-tracked additional route-miles. It operated 1,637 km of broad gauge, 3,665 km of meter gauge and 6,061 km of narrow gauge, all with 1,081 stations. It carried 496 million passengers.

As a measure of the depth to which the British influenced the railways of India, it wasn't until 2012 that the Great Indian Peninsula Railway Act of 1849 was repealed along with thirty-seven other railway-related acts of the same era. Although obsolete since the 1947 merger, these laws which had laid the foundations for the railroads had been on the books until they finally came to be recognized as unnecessary.

Today, Indian Railways maintain thirty-four museums, including the National Rail Museum in New Delhi and Regional Rail Museums at Chennai, Mysore, Howrah and Nagpur. In these museums, Indian Railways has preserved about two hundred thirty steam locomotives and a hundred ten vintage freight and passenger cars, many of which are more than a hundred years old. About sixteen of the preserved steam locomotives are maintained in working condition. At Rewari alone, there are six broad gauge and four meter gauge working steam locomotives including the iconic "Fairy Queen" (1855), the oldest working locomotive in the World.

Indian Railways also has preserved infrastructure. As of now, about twenty-five bridges and seventy buildings are designated as Heritage Assets by Indian Railways including Jubilee Bridge near Kolkata, Yamuna Bridge near Naini,

Sonenagar Bridge, Pamban viaduct, Bandra suburban station, Pratap Vilas Palace, Vadodara, Glenogle Bunglow, Mumbai SER (erstwhile BNR) Headquarters, and more.

In 2015, India's Union Council of Ministers approved a Japanese proposal for the nation's first high-speed railway. More or less predictably, however, the effort has been tied up in the courts ever since and little real progress has been made. As of 2020, India's fastest train is Train 18, unofficially named for the year of its introduction (2018), but officially known as the Vande Bharat Express. It runs between New Delhi and Varanasi, a distance of about four-hundred-twenty-five miles, at an average speed of sixty-three mph and with a maximum speed of ninety-nine mph.

Locomotives

India continued to use steam power long after most of the rest of the world had abandoned it because the country had ample coal supplies, low labor costs, and very limited access to oil. On the North Western Railway, coal was carried in between nine and sixteen hundred miles from the East Indian Railway because there were no workable coal deposits in the west. Oil from the Persian Gulf was also used but coal was competitive and was not replaced by the oil.

Locomotive builders were chosen by competitive bid with each railway managing its own bidding process so there were many requests for quote, many bids, and ultimately many locomotive manufacturers shipping to India. Almost all were British but the stew was spiced with a sprinkling of German and Swiss machines along with a few from other nations. 2-4-0 and 0-4-2 designs were popular at first and then 0-6-0 and 4-4-0 designs came into prominence.

While the initial EIR locomotives were built with inside cylinders, some with outside cylinders were made necessary by the introduction of the narrow gauge and their success led to the introduction of the 2-4-0 which soon became the most common type on the railroad. Stephenson or Allan valve gear was frequently used.

The Indians often added or enlarged cabs and cab roofs on the British locomotives for protection from the sun. Roofs were often double and lengthened to extend back over the fireman's working area. Cabs often included canvas curtains for further protection.

Locomotives delivered from Europe came in knocked down condition and were assembled at the shops in India. Spare parts were included and it was customary for a builder with an order for twenty or more locomotives to include enough spare parts to assemble an extra locomotive. This was the origin of the Indian locomotive industry. One locomotive was built in 1865 at the Byculla Works in Bombay but between then and 1941, only seven hundred more were built in India with some twelve thousand imported from Britain.

Early locomotive orders were well in excess of need, primarily because in the early days no one knew what the need would be and most wanted to play it safe. The early government profitability guarantee also contributed to the level of orders because more money invested in a railway automatically meant more profit. Many early locomotives went into storage on arrival and did not enter service until years later.

By 1869 there were 1,045 broad gauge locomotives in service on a total of ten railroads. The EIR had 466, the largest stable, with the GIPR rostering 264, the Madras 109 and the others much smaller numbers. Of this 1,045, 839 or a little more than ninety-one percent were six-wheel types: 2-4-0, 0-4-2, 2-2-2, or 0-6-0. Despite the broad gauge, all were relatively small and light.

The first locomotives on the EIR were a pair of 2-2-2 tank locomotives from Kitson & Co. in 1855. Notably, the last 2-2-2 type worked until 1908 and both of the first arrivals have survived and are now in museums. More of their ilk soon arrived and the EIR had forty in service by the end of the year, joined by about half as many 0-4-2s. Locomotive numbers were initially assigned in the order the locomotives were completed but that scheme didn't last long and soon the numbering became almost chaotic in its complexity. Two of the early 2-2-2s were diverted from railway duty to power boats on the Ganges but they were later returned to their flanged wheels and re-entered railway service. The 2-2-2s and 0-4-2s shared many parts and were an early example of the value of standardization.

The first eight GIPR locomotives were 2-4-0s from the Vulcan Foundry of Newton-le-Willows, England. They were shipped to India in 1852 and were soon supplemented by forty-three more of the same type from Kitson & Co. of Leeds. With a few small exceptions, the line ran exclusively with 2-4-0 types into the 1860s.

The Madras Railway, like many others, began life with a mixture of 2-4-0, 0-4-2 and 0-6-0 locomotives but, unusual for India, they were mostly wood-burners. Coal eventually replaced wood as a fuel but it took many years to do so.

The Eastern Bengal Railway began service with a group of inside-cylindered 2-4-0s but they were soon joined by 0-6-0s and 4-4-0s. After 1900, the line branched out buying 4-4-2, 4-4-2T, 2-6-4T and 4-6-0 locomotives but it was not until the late 1920s that the line bought 4-6-2 Pacifics and a small number of 2-8-2 Mikados and 0-8-0 switchers.

The earliest locomotives on the Oudh & Rohilkhand were a strange group of four 0-8-0 types built in 1865 by Sharp, Stewart & Co. of Manchester and Glasgow with intermediate crankshafts between the cylinders and the drivers. They were given non-English language names and were among the very few locomotives in the country to be so named.

On the North Western Railway, two 0-6-0 locomotives were placed back-to-back on either end of a common tender providing traction for heavily graded sections and eliminating the need for turnarounds at the end of a run. Articulated Garrets showed up on the Bengal-Nagpur Railway.

4-6-0s for freight appeared in the 1880s. Early 4-6-0s on the North Western were built in the 1880s in Scotland with Belpaire fireboxes but later ones were radial-stayed. The North Western "L" class 4-6-0s eventually numbered two hundred twenty-five locomotives with a boiler pressure of 160psi and fifty-one inch drivers. They achieved 23,784 pounds of tractive effort.

Experiments included compounding as early as 1883, a series of 2-2-2-0 locomotives, and at least one 2-4-0 with ninety-six inch drivers and triple expansion.

The BB&CIR's locomotives were very much in line with other railways' equipment in India: initially a group of outside cylindered 2-4-0s supplemented by 0-6-0s with inside cylinders. A few 2-6-0s were built in 1873 and, as was common, other wheel arrangements appeared and locomotives got heavier and more capable over the years. The BB&CIR Class D 4-4-0 locomotives were given names and it's indicative of the era that all the names were those of British Royalty; not an Indian in the whole lot. The Eastern Bengal Railway did the same with its late-1920s Pacifics, essentially all names beginning with "Lord" or "Sir" (as in "Lord Dalhousie" and "Sir John Shore"). The Bengal-Nagpur Railway also named a good many locomotives but its names were mostly descriptive with only a few (King Edward, for example) recalling people. The East Indian Railway followed the trend by naming most of its locomotives but records of the names were lost and now they are known for only twenty-six locomotives, all of which were purchased prior to 1860. The Madras & Southern Mahratta named at least sixty of its locomotives. A few were given names of Indian geographic features ("Brahmaputra," "Ganges," and "Godavari") and one was actually named after an Indian ("Ranjit Singh").

In 1880, an inventory of the EIR railroad's stores revealed the fact that there were sufficient spare parts on hand to construct a dozen new 2-4-0s and four new 0-6-0s, requiring only that boilers be made.

The 2.7% grades in the ghats were always a problem for the GIPR. After experimenting with 0-4-0 and 4-6-0 type tank engines, the line settled in 1865 on an 0-8-0 tank design and used it extensively for thirty years. Normal practice was to put two of these locomotives on every train, one at each end of the train when going uphill and both in front going downhill.

On the North Western, two German 0-6-2T Abt rack-and-pinion locomotives were purchased in 1887 to handle an especially steep grade in Bolan Pass. They worked that line for about a year but when a new alignment was built, they were set aside and then converted to conventional locomotives for switching duties. The following year, 1888, saw the purchase of ten 0-6-0 "twins," paired locomotives intended to run back to back against a common tender. Intended for heavy grades, the twins were not successful and were ultimately converted into more conventional locomotives. Also purchased in 1888 were four 0-8-0T tank locomotives that ultimately proved successful on the grades and led to the eventual use of 2-8-2T types.

In America and in Russia, where distances are long between stops, locomotives were designed for high power and speed. In Europe, where distances are shorter, they were designed more for acceleration and less for power. In India, locomotives tended to have characteristics between those two extremes. Given India's limited supply of high quality coal and almost non-existent supply of oil, the emphasis on locomotive design was toward the use of low-grade coal and (later) toward electric traction and not diesel.

An attempt had been made in 1872 to establish standard locomotive designs, hoping to reduce cost and improve delivery times from Britain, but that attempt failed because the various consulting engineers could not agree on many details. A scheme of class designations was devised in 1890 and a second, more successful attempt at defining standards was made in 1901 resulting in a standard passenger 4-4-0 and a standard freight 0-6-0. These designs, however, soon proved too light so they were supplemented by a standard 4-6-0, a standard 4-4-2 (for mail trains) and a standard 2-8-0 for heavy freight. By 1903 the standards seemed to have jelled and it was hoped that the number of classes in use could be reduced to less than fifty from the then-current quantity of nearly five hundred. Ultimately, however, the standard designs proved only a limited success: by 1906 still more variations were created including an alternative 2-6-0 design, a 2-6-4T, and others. In 1908 a general renumbering was undertaken to bring some sense to the roster. Notably all this work was done well in advance of any attempt at standardization in the USA which did not occur until it was forced by World War I after 1917.

In 1924 the issue of locomotive standardization in India was visited again, the results being influenced by the work that had been done in the United States by the US Railroad Administration. Indian Railway standards became the class XA (light 4-6-2), XB (moderate 4-6-2), XC (heavy 4-6-2), XD (light 2-8-2) and XE (heavy 2-8-2). Later added were classes XF and XG (light and heavy 0-6-0 switchers), XP and XS (experimental 4-6-2s), XT (0-4-2T) and XH (a very heavy 2-8-2). The XH was designed but was never built. The others, after some teething problems and a few serious accidents, were successful.

The "X" prefix on the class identifiers indicated broad gauge. There were also "Y" classes for meter gauge, "Z" classes for 2-foot 6-inch narrow gauge and "Q" classes for 2-foot 0-inch narrow gauge. After the war, a new 4-6-2 locomotive was designed and was given the classification "WP". In this case, the "W" replaced the "X" as a designator of the broad gauge and the "P" stood for "passenger." Similarly, a new 2-8-2 was designed using the same boiler and motion of the WP. Being intended for freight (goods) service, it was given the "WG" identifier.

The definition of standard locomotives for the narrow gauge (the Z class locomotives) had only minor impact on the scene because the roads failed to order them in significant quantities. Only the ZB (a 2-6-2) and the ZE (a 2-8-2) had any degree of popularity, the ZB selling forty-three copies and the ZE sixty.

Superheating, compounding, piston valves, outside cylinders and Walschaerts valve gear appeared in India mostly at the same time they appeared elsewhere in the world.

Superheating was introduced on the GIPR in 1912 and was applied to a group of 1907 class E1 4-4-2 Atlantics starting in 1925. Two Atlantics, numbers 909 and 922, had been renamed "President Taft" and "Roosevelt" in 1909 for use with a large party of visiting American tourists. The following year, the German Crown Prince visited and received similar treatment: number 924 became "Kron Prinz". In 1911, numbers 921 and 922 were given a coat of dark blue paint and were renamed "King Emperor" and "Queen Empress." Superheating was also introduced on the South Indian Railway in 1913 but only new locomotives were given superheaters and no attempt was made to upgrade earlier ones.

In 1906 the North British Locomotive Company built two deGlehn compound Atlantics (4-4-2s) on an experimental basis[10]. They were successful enough to warrant the construction of twelve more, becoming class KS after superheaters were applied. They served on the Bengal-Nagpur Railway as numbers 400-413 and all (except 411) lasted until 1949. The deGlehn Atlantics were followed by

---

[10] DeGlehn compound locomotives used uncoupled driving wheels and a mixture of inside and outside high and low pressure cylinders to power them. The deGlen system, while complex, was highly successful on the French Nord Railway and also ran successfully in Belgium, Germany and England.

a series of eighteen deGlehn Pacifics in 1929. The existence of the deGlehn locomotives and the use of Caprotti and Lentz poppet valve gears were departures from the Indian norm and were ultimately to make maintenance more and more difficult. The Indian North Western Railway also purchased a sampling of deGlehn compounds which ran from 1910 until 1927 but were considered only a marginal success because of the skill they required from the engineman to achieve their full potential.

The Bengal-Nagpur Railway was the only broad gauge Indian line to use Garratts (except for one experimental locomotive on the North Western). Two were purchased in 1925, each replacing a pair of 2-8-0 locomotives. Twenty six more were bought in 1930 and 1931 and a final four in 1939. Divided into four classes of varying weights to suit lines with varying rail, all had long service lives. The meter-gauge Assam-Bengal Railway purchased five 2-6-2+2-6-2 Garratts from Beyer-Peacock of Manchester, England in 1927.

In 1923, Baldwin provided a 2-6-6-2 Mallet and in 1925 Beyer Peacock a 2-6-2+2-6-2 Garrett. Both were tried out experimentally on the Bolan Pass grade by the North Western but both suffered from slipping, were costly to maintain, and were judged less successful than a pair of HG class 2-8-0 consolidations. They worked for some years, were taken out of service and stored, and then were scrapped in the late 1930s.

Early in the 1920s, some 4-6-2s and some 2-8-2s were built with wide fireboxes for use with lower-grade coal.

The 0-4-0 narrow gauge locomotives on the two foot gauge Darjeeling Himalayan Railway were unique and successful, A combination adhesion and rack locomotive on the Nilgiri Railway climbs 1:12.28 hills with a second set of cylinders to drive the rack wheels on the steepest sections. All four cylinders are outside the frame and when all four are working, the visual results are fascinating because the crankshafts rotate backwards in relation to the driving wheels.

Some class SPS 4-4-0 passenger locomotives had extremely long lives. Built in 1903, at least one was still working in Pakistan as late as the 1980s. They had Belpaire fireboxes, inside cylinders, flanged stacks, and six-wheel tenders.

The North Western's 0-8-0T locomotives were joined on the grades by a series of 2-8-4T and 0-8-4T locomotives and then, in 1916, a massive 2-10-0 tender locomotive was designed. It took time, but finally, in 1920, thirty of these locomotives were built and entered service. They were followed by a proposal for a still-larger 2-10-4 and a 2-8-0+0-8-2 Garratt, but those were never built.

In 1924, Baldwin shipped two 4-6-2 Pacifics and two 2-8-2 Mikados to the Madras Railway. Although successful (they served into the 1960s) they were not duplicated and were among a very small number of US-built locomotives in India. Early Madras & Southern Mahratta locomotives were painted green with white details but starting in 1898 a brick red was used and then in 1908 the color became black with polished zinc boiler bands.

A group of forty 4-4-2 Atlantics was transferred to the North Western from the GIPR. Built in 1907 by the North British Locomotive Company of Glasgow, they had been heavily modified in the late 1920s with the addition of superheaters, larger cylinders and outside steam pipes. On receipt by the North Western, they underwent further modification to move their trailing axles a foot further back and to install Skefco roller-bearing outside axle boxes. Twenty four of the forty also received new frames.

Thirty 2-10-0 locomotives of the N class were purchased by the North Western in 1936. They were oil fired and were capable of moving longer and heavier trains than any other locomotives on the line's one percent grades. In 1942, in a drive to make greater use of available locomotives, the N class was converted to burn coal. Since the fireboxes were eleven feet long, mechanical stokers by the Standard Stoker Company of the USA were installed.

At the other end of the spectrum were the XT class 0-4-2T locomotives. With Caprotti valve gear, they had been built by the Essen works of Friedrich Krupp in Germany and were capable of 11,088 pounds of tractive effort. Easy on the rails and nimble, the XTs were handy when trains were short.

One of the dominant locomotives on the meter-gauge lines was the class F 0-6-0 which was purchased and put into service from 1875. A total of 1,035 of these were built up to 1922 with only minor variation in dimensions. The first class Fs proved a little too heavy for the light track so subsequent ones were scaled back, the thirteen-and-a-half inch cylinders being reduced to thirteen inches, the boiler reduced in size, and wheelbase reduced from five foot nine inchs to an even five feet.

After some experimentation, the Kandahar Railway settled on its "L" class 4-6-0 locomotives but in 1928 they began to be replaced by 4-6-2 Pacifics and by 2-8-2 tank locomotives. The ultimate solution on the Sind Peshin State Railway turned out to be the railway's standard 2-8-0 tender locomotives, most of which had been built by the Vulcan Foundry at Newton-le-Willows in Lancashire.

Broad gauge railway mileage was 4,241 in 1869 and 13,901 in 1900. The number of broad gauge railways had increased to twelve and the total of locomotives in service to 3,049. In addition to the common six-wheel types, there were then 654 4-4-0s, 104 2-6-0s and 322 4-6-0s. By 1920 there were a total of 5,904 locomotives in service, with the most common wheel arrangement being the 0-6-0 (2,128 locomotives) followed at a distance by the 4-4-0 (847), the 4-6-0 (812), the 2-8-0 (916) and various tank locomotives (827).

The introduction of heavier and more powerful locomotives combined with the reduced traffic brought on by the depression served to reduce the number in service. In 1940, a total of nine railways reported 5,302 locomotives, some ten percent less than in 1920. The 0-6-0 wheel arrangement remained the most numerous (at 1,447) but the 2-8-0 arrangement was a close second (at 1,367). 4-6-0s and 4-6-2s were also common (654 and 314 respectively) but tank locomotives of all wheel arrangements were more common, numbering nine hundred.

In addition, several hundred locomotives worked at the ports in Bombay, Calcutta, and elsewhere and at industries spread across the country. They were predominantly 0-4-0T and 0-6-0T designs but a few larger and more powerful locomotives appeared in the mix. For instance, a pair of 2-10-2T switchers was built for the Bombay Port Trust in 1922 by Nasmyth, Wilson & Co. of Manchester; a lone 0-8-0 was built in 1935 by Hunslet Engine Co. of Leeds for Tata Iron & Steel. The Tata 0-8-0, number 24, had footboards that ran the length of the tender on both side to facilitate moving large numbers of switchmen around the plant and its yard.

As was true elsewhere in the world, industry in the first part of the twentieth century in India often handled internal material movement issues with private internal railroads. Because these railroads had to squeeze between buildings and sometimes between machines inside buildings, and because they only rarely interchanged freight with the public railroads that served the plants, the private railroads were often built to narrow gauge: in the USA to 36-inch gauge and in India to either 2-foot 6-inch gauge or to 2-foot gauge. No detailed accounting exists but prior to World War II, based on what is known, something over a thousand narrow gauge locomotives by more than forty manufacturers worked in industrial India for more than two hundred firms. Although there were a few larger and heavier ones, the great majority were either 0-4-0 or 0-6-0 in either a tank or tender version.

Beginning in 1940, the Indian Government began ordering locomotives in bulk and began numbering them in a single series irrespective of the line for which they were intended.

In total, some ten thousand broad gauge steam locomotives served in India (and Ceylon) between 1851 and 1940. Ninety-four percent of them were built by British manufacturers, two-and-a-half percent in India from parts by British manufacturers, and the remaining three-and-a-half percent by Europeans and Americans. Record-keeping was detailed, in large part because the government profit guarantees required it.

Many Indian locomotives, being designed and built by the British, featured typically British design elements: Belpaire fireboxes were common as they were in Britain; Running boards were frequently lowered below the tops of the drivers and fenders (what the British call "splashers") were provided to protect the crew from the moving wheels. Later and larger locomotives had higher running boards and often radial-stayed fireboxes but the persistence of coupling buffers and chains continued to give the locomotives a British appearance.

About a thousand Class YG 2-8-2 Mikados were built from 1949 to 1972 by a variety of manufacturers for meter-gauge freight service; three are preserved in working order at the Rewari Steam Locomotive Shed southwest of Delhi. Ten Class WL light Pacifics were built by the Vulcan Foundry (UK) and ninety-four by the Chittaranjan Locomotive Works for broad gauge branch lines. Number 15005, Sher-e-Punjab, is preserved at Rewari.

And, in 1941, the class WL Pacifics arrived. These locomotives had sixty-seven inch drivers, thirty-eight square feet of grate area, a working pressure of two hundred ten psi, superheaters, thermic syphons, and pedal-operated Ajax steam butterfly doors.

During World War II, locomotives were taken from India to serve in the Middle East. Emergency orders were placed with both Baldwin and the Canadian Locomotive Company and something like six hundred sixty locomotives were imported into India as a result. These locomotives, built to American standards and practices, had significant influence on future locomotive designs in India. They had bar frames, outside cylinders, alligator-type crossheads and cast tender trucks. Paid for by the United States, they were free to the Indian railways that accepted them and were ultimately quite successful.

In 1943 the US Army Transportation Corps also delivered a little more than four hundred Alco-designed 2-8-2 meter gauge steam locomotives, mostly to the

Assam-Bengal Railway. After the war, they simply stayed there, forming the backbone of the post-war meter gauge system. Most had been built by Alco or Baldwin but a few had come from Davenport, Porter and Vulcan (of Pennsylvania, not to be confused with the British Vulcan locomotive firm). Thirty-three more were built by Baldwin and received in 1948. Beyer Peacock also supplied twenty-seven 2-8-0+0-8-2, two dozen 2-8-2+2-8-2, and eighteen 4-8-2+-2-8-4 Garratt locomotives between 1943 and 1945. At some point, probably during shopping, builder's plates were removed from the meter-gauge Mikados and then re-installed on the wrong locomotives resulting in an Alco machine, for instance, carrying a Baldwin builder's plate. Confusion was the order of the day.

After World War II, a severe locomotive shortage caused more orders to be placed with both Canadian and US manufacturers. The Canadian Locomotive Works and the Montreal Locomotive Works together shipped 437 broad gauge 2-8-2 Mikado-types and the Baldwin Locomotive Works another 164 of a nearly identical design. Baldwin later shipped another sixty copies plus forty of a somewhat larger version. In addition, General Electric shipped thirty center-cab diesel switchers.

India was not excused from the mania for streamlining that resulted in locomotives like the Norfolk & Western J-class, the New York Central's Commodore Vanderbilt, the Reading's Crusader, and others across the United States, Europe and Australia. The North Western spent some time and money dressing up a few locomotives for special occasions. An 'L' class 4-6-0 was converted from its normal black with polished steel boiler bands to Great Western green with black and yellow trim. Pacific 4-6-2 number 240 appeared in Midland red and her sister number 1855 in brown lined in black and yellow. The BB&CIR initially painted its locomotives green but by 1900 they had become black although in 1938 some were painted chocolate with yellow stripes on the cab and tender for mail service.

Elephant ears (smoke lifters) were applied to at least some of the Western Railway's YP class 4-6-2 Pacifics and some of the Southern Railway's YG class 2-8-2 Mikados.

The Central Railway's WP class of 4-6-2 Pacifics included a number of locomotives built with modest streamlining in place. They were given domed smokebox fronts with centered headlights and eight-point stars painted around the headlights; they had skyline casings that hid their domes and most boiler-top appliances, and they had tiny, vestigial bits of skirting, primarily beside the steps that ran from the running boards to the pilot beams. The locomotives, of course, were used in passenger service.

In the thirties and again after World War II, a variety of handsome streamlined Pacifics (4-6-2) saw passenger service on the North Western Railway.

Another group of Indian Railways Pacifics was built by the Chittaranjan Locomotive Works between 1963 and 1967. They carried 210 psi of steam, had sixty-seven inch drivers and achieved in-service speeds in excess of sixty mph. Built with a skyline casing along the top of the boiler, bullet nose in front, a headlight centered on that bullet, and an eight-pointed sheet-metal star surrounding the headlight, they also featured a most usual polished brass crown atop their stacks. The Class WP required a crew of three to operate including two firemen who were needed to handle the huge amounts of coal the locomotive burned. A total of 259 were built.

In 1939 a class of four 4-6-2 Pacifics were built by Vulcan for the North Western Railway with full streamlining: aluminum covers, bullet noses with centered, recessed headlights, skyline casings, aprons, skirting and painted red stripes centered on the skirting. Other Pacifics were built by Baldwin in 1947 for the East Indian Railway, by Canadian Locomotive Company in 1949 and by Chittaranjan Locomotive Works in 1965 with lesser amounts of streamlining: bullet noses with recessed and centered headlights, clean boilers and skyline casings but no or little skirting, a standard non-matching tender and no shiny aluminum.

Meter gauge Pacifics were also purchased in 1948 but they were bought without any streamlining at all. The locomotive committee had discouraged streamlining on the broad gauge locomotives but had been overruled by the Railway Board which felt that its public appeal warranted the extra purchase and maintenance costs. But the locomotive committee apparently won the argument for the meter gauge locomotives.

As of 1981, the smallest locomotives working on the Indian Railways were a group of four 2-4-0T side tankers built for the 2-foot 6-inch gauge, one by W G Bagnall in 1927, another also by Bagnall in 1936, and two by Yorkshire Engine in 1933. They each weigh in at 11.8 tons.

At peak, in the middle 1960s, the Indian Railways had 10,711 steam locomotives in service of which 6,668 were broad gauge, 3,645 meter gauge, and 398 narrow gauge. By 1994 that total had fallen to 911 and by 2007, only fifty remained for special service.

In total, something like 33,000 locomotives saw service on the Indian Railways before 1990. Almost half of them had been built before 1941. Today, India uses electric and diesel locomotives, along with a few CNG (compressed natural gas) locomotives and steam locomotives run only to pull heritage trains. Loco-

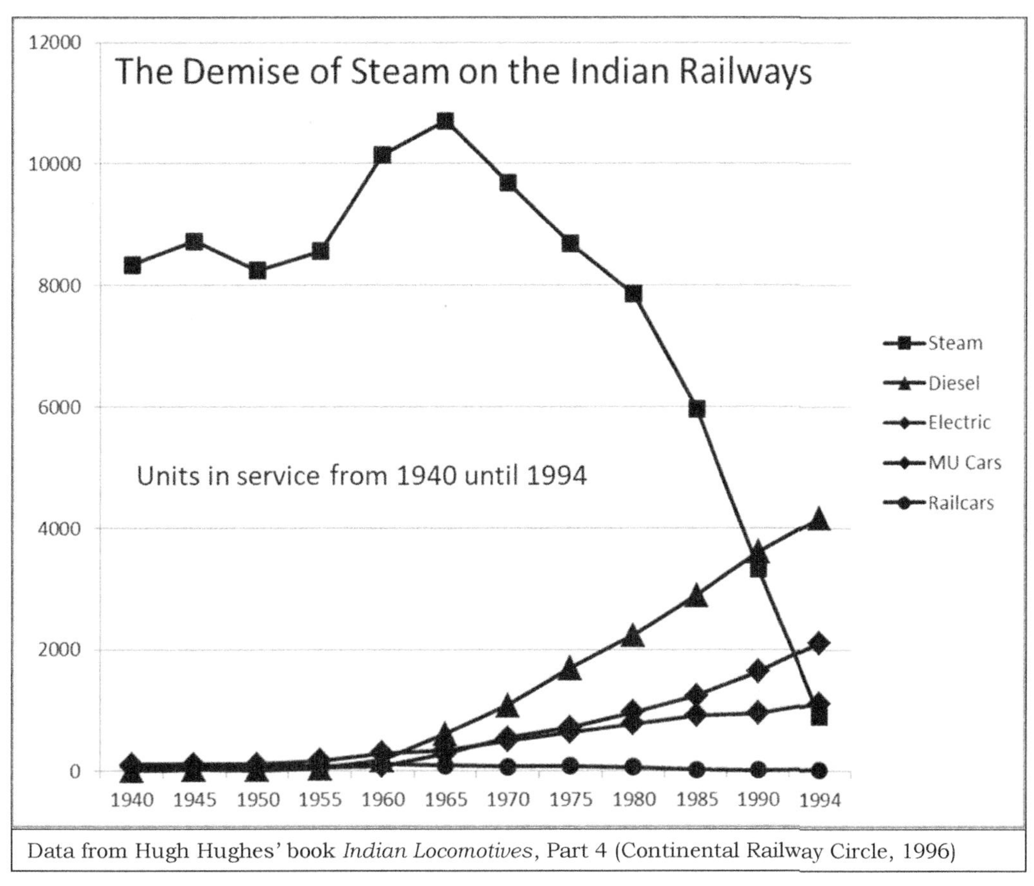

Data from Hugh Hughes' book *Indian Locomotives*, Part 4 (Continental Railway Circle, 1996)

motives in India are assigned a four- or five-letter classification code. The first letter denotes the track gauge; the second their motive power (diesel or electric), and the third their assignment (freight, passenger, multiple or switching). The fourth letter denotes a locomotive's chronological model number and the fifth, where it is used, indicates a newer diesel locomotive's horsepower range or, in some cases, a technical variant in a class. In the 2004-2005 fiscal year, Indian Railways had 4,801 diesel locomotives and 3,065 electric locomotives on its roster.

The North Western purchased a single steam-powered railcar from the Vulcan Foundry (of England) in 1905 and three more from the Sentinel Wagon Works (of England) in 1926. Three two-car steam articulated sets built by Sentinel Wagon Works arrived from the GIPR in 1933.

In 1930 the North Western received two Beardmore diesel-electrics for branch line service and in 1935 two larger Armstrong-Sulzer units arrived for Karachi-Lahore passenger service. All had been set aside before World War II started.

Another diesel was delivered to the Bombay, Baroda & Central India in 1936 by Armstrong Whitworth of Newcastle, England. Dieselization began on the North Western in 1939 with the purchase of eleven Ganz diesel-mechanical railcars. These cars turned out to have been poorly made and they gave so much trouble that a complete rebuild was required with the first car going into the shop in October 1940. The rebuild corrected many manufacturing flaws and helped extend the life of the railcars but did not convince management that dieselization was the wave of the future. Two other railcars and three diesel-electric locomotives met with similar problems.

In 1939 the Nizam State Railway purchased four diesel-mechanical railcars from the Drewery Car Company of London. Each seated 84 passengers, was powered by a six-cylinder 82 hp Gardner engine on each truck and was air conditioned.

In 1944 and 1945 by a group of fifteen B-B diesels from General Electric went to the Western Railroad (and subsequently some of them to the Eastern). Designed for switching service, they had problems of their own but were considered overall to be successful and ultimately led to serious dieselization after the 1947 partition. In 1954, the door swung open and diesels began to arrive: from Krauss-Maffei twenty went to the Central and ten more to the Northern. They were followed by a Niagara of locomotives from EMD, Alco and, increasingly, from the Indian Railway's own Diesel Locomotive Works and the Chittaranjan Works.

The first meter gauge diesel came when Brookville of Pennsylvania delivered a single small 4-wheel switcher to the Jamnagar & Dwarka Railway in 1940. John Fowler of Leeds, England delivered a half-dozen three axle units in 1949, also to the JDR. The first meter-gauge electrics arrived on the South Indian Railway in 1930 when Hawthorn Leslie and English Electric shipped four B-B units to the Southern.

The first meter gauge main line diesels were a group of twenty ordered in 1953 for the Western Railway's Palanpur-Kandla line which had serious water problems. They came from the North British Locomotive Company of Glasgow. Later purchases came from Alco, EMD, Montreal and, starting in 1968, from India's Diesel Locomotive Works.

The narrow gauge lines (2-foot and 2-foot 6-inch) held onto their steam power much longer than their big brothers. They continued to order new steam locomotives as late as 1959 and did not receive any diesels until 1955 when Jung of Jungenthal, Germany shipped eight diesel-hydraulics for use on the Central and Northern Railways. The three Central Railway units were 2-foot gauge and were designed to handle grades of up to five percent and curves as sharp as fifteen meter radius on the Matheran line. The other five were 2-foot 6-inch gauge for the Kalka-Simla route. Then, in 1964, Maschinenbau of Kiel, Germany shipped twenty-five more B-B diesel hydraulics to India. Ten were 2-foot gauge and fifteen were 2-foot 6-inch gauge.

The first electrics appeared in 1925 in Bombay suburban service. Dieselization and electrification, however, didn't seriously begin until the mid-1950s. By 1972, steam was down to thirty percent of freight ton-miles.

The BB&CI purchased two battery-electric switching locomotives (numbers 901-902) in 1927 and a six-wheel diesel (number 800) in 1936. The electrics were bought to work in the newly-electrified commuter district together with forty 4-car multiple-unit sets.

The first mainline electrification in India was done on the GIPR between Bombay and Poona. Twenty two more 1Co2 locomotives and 41 C-C locomotives were built between 1928 and 1930 for that service.

The earliest electric locomotives were 2-C-2 boxcabs, three of which were delivered to the GIPR in 1928-29 by Hawthorn Leslie of Newcastle, England and twenty more in 1930 by Schweizerische Locomotive & Machine of Winterthur, Switzerland. They were built for fifteen hundred volt DC catenary and placed in service starting in 1930. One, number 4006, is preserved at the National Rail Museum in New Delhi. In 1928 Schweizerische also delivered ten copies of a C-C "crocodile" design similar to many others built for use in Switzerland and the next year, Vulcan delivered thirty-one almost-identical units.

By 1941 there were ninety-three broad gauge electric MU cars in suburban service around Bombay on the GIPR and BB&CIR. Fifty-six more were added in 1951-53 with British, German, Swiss and Italian builders but, starting in 1958, India began building its own EMU cars in factories in Calcutta and Perambur. By 1983 there were over eight hundred units in service.

The Central Railway (Scindia line) received three B-B 2-foot gauge electric locomotives from Bharat Heavy Electrical Works of Jhansi, India in 1987.

Cars

Early in the nineteenth century there was no canal system in India and what roads existed were poorly built and only seasonally useable. The railroads thus had little competition and an incentive to keep freight rates high. Coal moved from Raniganj to Calcutta by rail and then to Bombay by boat rather than going across the nation by the all-rail route. Especially on the west coast, imported English coal remained cheaper than domestic supplies that had to come across the subcontinent by rail. The immediate result was that India remained primarily an agricultural nation. The government began to set maximum freight rates in 1862 and by 1887 had essentially completed the job.

Early freight cars were largely 4-wheel. Buffers and screw couplings were used according to British practice. In 1900 most freight moved in cars with six ton tare and twelve ton capacity. By the 1970s, there were still many 4-wheel cars in use but bogies were becoming more common.

Following World War I, the annual demand for new freight cars was estimated to be eight thousand and it was thought that that demand would continue for many years to come. As of March 2017, the Indian Railway freight car fleet consisted of 277,987 units.

One class of meter gauge and narrow gauge cars looks in photographs for all the world like they were made from B&O wagontop box cars: they have vertical side ribs which extend over the roof without an eave. The cars appear windowless and thus are probably material cars and not coaches although the photographs show them in passenger trains. They appeared on the Nilgiri mountain railway, the Jodhpur-Bikaner Railway, and the Gaekwar's Baroda State Railway.

The very earliest passenger cars were small, 4-wheel lightweight cars, kept small because there were no switching locomotives. Lightweight cars could be moved about the terminals by a gang of men pushing while the heavier and larger six-wheel cars and those on four-wheel trucks could not. Even the earliest cars, however, had glass windows in first and second class to help control interior temperatures in the heat of tropical India.

In response to overcrowding, the GIPR introduced bi-level passenger cars in 1862. The cars had a capacity of 120 people each but had such low ceilings that standing was impossible. Other double-deck cars provided roomier accommodations above and restricted spaces intended for servants on the lower level. Complaints about traveling conditions continued, however, centering on crowding and on the lack of on-board toilet facilities. Lavatories were installed in third-class carriages starting in 1891.

Mail was carried and sorted en-route in special cars starting in 1864, only two years after sorting in motion began on specialized railroad cars in the USA.

Fourth class passenger service, introduced in 1874, at first included no seating but benches were added beginning in 1885 when the Intermediate class was introduced and fourth was renamed third. There were then four classes: First, Second, Inter and Third. On some trains there were also cars reserved for women at all class levels. First class cars were denoted with leather curtains on the windows. Both first and second class cars had double roofs while third and fourth classes did not. Generally, inter-line through cars were limited to first and second classes; the inter and third class passengers had to change cars.

Since wood was readily available, rolling stock was made locally to British designs. A full-size pattern would be shipped from England and copied in India. Sunshades and double roofs were early features of passenger cars due to the heat. The first steel underframes were used in 1885. Vacuum brakes were adopted starting in 1879. Imported bogie 4-wheel trucks and electrical lighting began to appear in 1903. The Pullman standard section, as it was known in the USA, was never used in India.

In the 1860s, first and second class travel in India was approximately equal in comfort to those classes in Britain and, on the broad gauge railways, the compartments were spacious. A first class compartment for four people measured about 8 by 12 feet with Pullman-style sofas that converted into beds at night and had an attached private lavatory and a small room for a servant. Mechanical air conditioning didn't exist on the railways until 1936 but other forms of cooling were tried with varying success. The trains, however, were notoriously slow and seemingly never ran on schedule.

Interestingly, the introduction of the railways in India forced people of different castes to ride together on the trains. Because there were poor Brahmins and (relatively) wealthy Pariahs, the separation of the people by their ability to pay for an expensive ticket didn't serve to separate the classes.

Military use of the railroads was important. In 1887 at the Lahore shops, an armored train was built. Equipped with artillery pieces and machine guns, it was tested but never used in actual fighting.

There were no private-owner cars on the Indian railways. Vacuum brakes were used on trains but in the later years, compressed air was used on diesel and electric locomotives. By the turn of the century, about half of the passenger car fleet had brake piping and ultimately the vacuum brakes were replaced with air brakes.

Passenger speeds were low – the fastest averaging up to 35 mph. Meter and narrow gauge trains were slower. In the mid-1930s, the Deccan Queen (on the GIPR) ran for sixty-two miles at 52 mph. Passenger trains offered no on-board food service due to caste and religious strictures; trains stopped for meals instead.

In the years before World War I, food orders from first class passengers were gathered by the carriage attendant in advance, telegraphed ahead, and the food brought to the passengers when the train came into the station. Everyone other than the first class passengers had to get off and run into the depot for a meal. This advanced telegraphing of food orders is reminiscent of what Fred Harvey had been doing in the USA for many years, although Harvey didn't restrict his services to the first class passengers and didn't deliver meals to his customers on board the train.

The introduction of diners started about 1901 and eventually there were both Hindu and Muslim refreshment cars containing both vegetarian and non-vegetarian kitchens. Since there were few vestibule and corridor cars, movement to and from the diners could occur only at stops.

After World War II, in the 1960s and 1970s, passenger services were plagued by overcrowding caused by insufficient rolling stock and line capacity and contributed to by inadequate terminal facilities in some places. The Indian railroads carried 2,431 million passengers in 1970-71, about ten percent of which was commuter traffic.

Mechanical air conditioning was introduced to the Indian Railways in 1956 but the first fully air-conditioned train (the Rajdhani Express between New Delhi and Howrah) was not introduced until 1969. Not only was the Rajdhani Express air-conditioned, it was the first in India to regularly run at speeds above sixty mph. Non-air conditioned cars remained in service into the early years of the 21st Century.

Twenty-four high speed coaches capable of a hundred sixty kilometers per hour (ninety-nine mph) were received from Alstom in 2001 and 2002 and as a result line speeds have increased but not to the extent of the high-speed trains of Europe or Japan.

On long distance routes and also on some shorter routes, the Indian Railway uses two primary types of coaches: ICF coaches, in production from 1955 until 2018 and LHB coaches which are lighter, safer and are capable of speeds up to a hundred sixty kilometers per hour (ninety-nine mph). Two new self-propelled train set designs were introduced in 2018. Known as Train-18 and Train-20, they are expected to replace locomotive-hauled trains on long distance routes. On regional short distance routes, Indian Railway runs Mainline Electrical Multiple Unit (MEMU) or Diesel Electrical Multiple Unit (DEMU) trains, depending on the traction available. Locomotive-hauled passenger trains having frequent stops are slowly being replaced with MEMU and DEMU train sets across India. On suburban commuter routes around the large urban centers, Indian Railway runs trains almost exclusively with Electric Multiple Unit (EMU) coaches. As of March 2017, about 9100 such coaches are in operation.

Facilities

India is a nation with many large cities and each has its own railroad station. As elsewhere, the largest cities required the largest stations and the smallest, little more than a shack next to a short platform. The station at Lahore resembled a medieval castle and was, in fact, designed to be defensible; trains could be driven into it and heavy doors closed over the tracks. Turrets provided shooting positions and archery windows gave the building atmosphere.

The largest and grandest of India's stations is Victoria Terminus in Bombay. Begun in 1852, it was formally opened on Victoria's Jubilee Day in 1887, a semi-gothic pile of millions of bricks featuring ornamented arches in rows and tiers along with corner towers and a cathedral-like central dome.

The city's first public building, Victoria Terminus was designed by Frederick William Stevens who styled his creation to merge Victorian Italianate Gothic Revival and traditional Indian architecture. Stevens worked closely with Indian craftsmen to build authentic features such as the many overhanging enclosed balconies. Inside the building, the architectural details are intricate. The main booking office is known as the Star Chamber for the star-covered white panels sitting between dark wood ribs in its ceiling. Columns of Indian stone and polished red and grey Italian marble topped with elaborate carvings of flowers, plants and animals support stunning vaulted ceilings and pointed Gothic arches. Now known as Chhatrapati Shivaji Terminus, the station's eighteen platforms remain in use today.

Railroads require shops where the locomotives and cars can be serviced and, when necessary, where they can be fixed. And in the days of steam, the shops were even more integral to the operation because a great deal more servicing was required. Shops were thus established on the GIPR at Byculla in 1854, on the BB&CIR at Amroli in 1856, and on the EIR at Howrah by 1853. In 1862 much larger shops were built at Jamalpur on the EIR and at Parel on the GIPR. These early shops were the first introduction of industry in the rural countryside so they accelerated economic progress and brought new ways of living and working to the people. The shops were also the first introduction of non-owner business management outside of the government. They employed people whose profession was management but who did not own the businesses and this added another major cultural shift.

It was thirty years before the Indian railroads began to expand the work their shops did from simple servicing and repair to the manufacture of new locomotives. Steam locomotive production started in 1885 at Jamalpur on the EIR broad gauge and in 1896 at Ajmer on the BB&CIR meter gauge. The shops at Jamalpur were huge since the land was provided by the government and thus was free to the railway. They were located in a previously isolated area, in part, because that would allow management to develop a workforce that would not be tempted by alternative employment and would thus be more stable and more tractable. By 1906, close to ten thousand were employed at Jamalpur.

The North Western originally built its shops on a hundred twenty-six acres in the city of Naulakha and by the early 1890s they employed four thousand. But that site became too small so the North Western built new shops on a thousand acres in the city of Lahore at Moghulpura. The new car shop opened in 1910 and the new locomotive shop in 1914. The complex included housing for the workers, all graded and segregated by caste and rank.

The production of steel in India began in 1911 and by 1929 the Indian Railways were no longer importing rails, chairs or fishplates, those items being made entirely in India.

By 1914 there were ninety-one railway workshops which employed 113,000 workers. During World War I, the shops stopped manufacturing exclusively for the railways and became war producers Some plants made ammunition including everything from bullets to hand grenades to large-diameter shells, others built horse-drawn wagons, ambulances and other vehicles in addition to their railway work; still others did other manufacturing, all contributing to the ultimate successful conclusion of the war.

The Peninsular Locomotive Company, a private enterprise intended to make locomotives, was proposed shortly after the completion of World War I but it failed to receive any encouragement from the government and soon folded.

After independence from Britain in 1948, India quickly developed its own internal locomotive manufacturing industry. As of the day of independence, ninety-one percent of all broad gauge locomotives and seventy-seven percent of the meter gauge ones had come from Britain. Only two-and-three-quarter percent of the broad gauge and eleven percent of the meter gauge had been made in India. It had been, indeed, a colonial captive market. But after independence, that changed.

Starting in 1947, the Chittaranjan Locomotive Works (and the new city of Chittaranjan) was built a little more than a hundred miles northwest of Calcutta. The works were originally planned to be built in the city of Chandmari but after the completion of World War II and the partition of India, it was thought that Chandmari was too close to the Pakistan border being less than two hundred miles from it. So the works were actually built at Chittaranjan, more than four hundred miles from what was then East Pakistan and is now Myanmar (Burma).

Chittaranjan was equipped to build locomotives almost solely from raw materials and it became India's prime supplier. The facility began producing locomotives in 1950 and produced the last steam locomotives (a group of sixty meter gauge 2-8-2s) in February 1972. Chittaranjan had been making electric locomotives since 1959 and it subsequently became Indian Railways' primary electric shop and also began to produce diesels. The plant covered more than two hundred acres of land and included a galvanizing shop, a steel foundry, a motor shop and more. Employment in the middle 1990s was about seventeen thousand five hundred.

The Diesel Locomotive Works was established at Varanasi (Benares) in 1961 with the first locomotives, an Alco design produced under license from Alco, completed in January 1964. A carriage shop, the Integral Coach Factory, opened in the Madras suburb of Perambur in 1955 and was the largest such plant in Asia, employing over fifteen thousand in the 1990s. A second Diesel Locomotive Works opened in Yelahanka near Bangalore in 1984. Although Indian Railways produces its own locomotives and passenger cars, freight cars are still made by outside firms to Indian Railway specifications.

As of the 21st century, Indian Railways operates a number of major locomotive manufacturing facilities:

- Chittaranjan Locomotive Works in Chittaranjan, West Bengal manufactures electric locomotives
- Diesel Locomotive Works in Varanasi, Uttar Pradesh manufactures diesel and electric locomotives
- Diesel Locomotive Factory in Marhowra, Bihar, a joint venture of Indian Railways and General Electric, manufactures high capacity diesel locomotives, used primarily for freight
- Electric Locomotive Factory in Madhepura, Bihar, a joint venture of Indian Railways and Alstom SA, manufactures electric locomotives

- Diesel-Loco Modernization Works in Patiala, Punjab upgrades and overhauls locomotives and manufactures electric locomotives

Important passenger car manufacturing facilities include the Integral Coach Factory in Chennai, Tamilnadu, the Rail Coach Factory in Kapurthala, Punjab, and the Modern Coach Factory in Raebareli, Uttar Pradesh. Indian Railways also operates rail and wheel factories in Bangalore, Karnataka and Chhapra, Bihar, forty-four locomotive sheds, two hundred twelve carriage and wagon repair units and forty-five periodic overhaul workshops.

Later Railways

Early traffic on the Indian railways more than fulfilled expectations. All the early lines were profitable (except the luckless Calcutta & Southeastern Railway which failed in 1868 and was subsequently taken over by the government) but only the GIPR and EIR made five percent so the government was forced to contribute.

In 1868 there were four thousand route miles of track. The opening of the Suez Canal in 1869 greatly reduced the cost of importing equipment and supplies and thus made subsequent construction easier. In fact, relationships between Britain and India and plans for railroad construction had been one of the factors that led to British involvement in the canal project. It, in turn, led to significant expansion of the rail network through the 1870s, 1880s and well into the twentieth century. By 1921 there were 175 railroads in India and by 1937 the number of route miles had grown to forty-three thousand.

In addition to the Indian Government and some private interests, railroads were

In 1943 the Indian Railways purchased a group of broad gauge 2-8-2 Mikado-type locomotives from the Montreal Locomotive Works because British locomotive suppliers were overwhelmed with war orders. Eighteen were delivered in 1943, fifty-two in 1944, and a hundred seventy-seven in 1945. The class locomotive, shown here in this Montreal builder's photo, was initially given the road number M-1, was later renumbered 5501, and still later became number 71187. It had 60-inch drivers, an engine weight of 198,000 pounds and a tractive force of 35,000 pounds; cylinders were 21 x 28 inches; steam pressure was 200 pounds Owned by the state railway, M-1 could have served almost anywhere on the system but she ended up working primarily on the Assam-Bengal Railway. [Author collection]

built by a variety of Princes, Maharajas and other local rulers and authorities. Known as the "Princely State" railways, they totaled about seven thousand miles. The Government also offered encouragement to private builders by forcing the main lines to share feeder traffic revenue with them.

There is the question of whether enough railways were built in India. One way to judge is to compare it with other nations. Using 1976 statistics, in total route mileage, the USA led the world with 281,000. The USSR came in second with 85,900, and India was well down the list with a little less than 38,000. If

Development of the broad gauge lines in India. Only the most significant routes are shown.

we considered route mileage per million acres of land area, Switzerland came out on top with over 3,000, the USA had 890 and India had 457. Or, if we considered route mileage per million of population, Australia had the most at almost 1,900; the USA had just half that at 950, and India, being heavily populated, had only 62. The reader can draw his or her own conclusions but it does appear that there was and still is room for railroad growth in India.

Broad Gauge Lines

The most extensive and most important construction in the last half of the nineteenth century was devoted to the broad gauge railways which were effectively the mainlines of India. In addition to the five roads described in this book as "early construction," at least eight other important broad-gauge Indian Railways date from the last half of the nineteenth century and later and are worthy of mention:

Great Southern Railway of India

The Great Southern Railway of India ran for seventy-eight miles from Negapatam through Trichinopoly to Erode. Opened in 1862 as far as Trichinopoly, it was completed to Erode in 1868 and was ultimately taken over by the government. The Great Southern became the South Indian Railway in 1874 and was converted to meter gauge. Portions, including the line between Erode and Trichinopoly, were converted back to broad gauge in 1929.

Madras & Southern Mahratta Railway

In 1908 the Madras & Southern Mahratta Railway was formed as a successor to the Madras Guaranteed Railway and the Southern Mahratta Railway.

That year, construction north from Calicut reached Mangalore on India's western coast. A line extending seven hundred miles further north along the coast to Bombay seemed obvious but was made difficult by the terrain and funding was hard to find. It was not until the 1990s that construction began on a line north from Mangalore to Roha, about two-thirds of the way to Bombay. The line was completed and opened in 1998 featuring something like eighteen hundred bridges and fifty-two miles of tunnels. Running along the coast as it does, the Konkan line (as it is called) crosses many rivers and tunnels through many rock spurs but climbs little. Its ruling gradient is a modest 0.7% and its maximum curvature is 1.4 degrees so the government hoped to work it at speeds of up to a hundred miles per hour. Notably, most of the construction work was motorized and little earth was carried by hand in baskets as had been the case in earlier construction projects.

Eastern Bengal Railway

The Eastern Bengal Railway was chartered in 1857 and intended to carry on to Dacca. A hundred-ten miles from Calcutta to Kushtia opened in 1862. In 1884 it was taken over by the state and merged with the Eastern Bengal Guaranteed Railway, the South Eastern Railway, and the North Bengal State Railway. In 1905 it was merged with the Bengal Central Railway. With completion of the Lower Ganges Bridge in 1915, much of the line was broad-gauged and re-gauging continued in pieces through 1926. In 1942 it was further merged with the meter gauge system of the Assam-Bengal Railway to form the Bengal & Assam Railway which operated as a dual-gauge corporation until 1952.

Calcutta & Southeastern Railway

Calcutta & Southeastern Railway ran from Calcutta to Canning, twenty-nine miles. It failed and was taken over by the government in 1868.

Indian Midland Railway

The Indian Midland ran from Itarsi to Jabalpur. It's completion in 1870 closed the transcontinental link and allowed, for the first time, all-rail travel between Calcutta and Bombay spanning the entire Indian sub-continent. The Indian Midland was merged into the GIPR in 1900.

Khyber Railway

The Khyber Railway was built in what is now Pakistan between 1919 and 1925 primarily as a defense against possible invasion from Afghanistan and the west. From Peshawar where there was an existing railroad, it ran west to Landi Kotal and beyond to the Afghanistan line. The terrain was mountainous so many switchbacks and tunnels were used.

Bengal Nagpur Railway

Work began on the Bengal Nagpur Railway in 1887 with construction between Asansol and Purulia (fifty miles) completed late in 1889. In 1888 some meter gauge segments that had been built earlier were converted to broad gauge and the whole length of the line from Asansol to Nagpur (six hundred thirty-seven miles) was completed by 1891. The BNR's formation included the taking over of the meter-gauge Nagpur-Chhattisgarh State Railway which had started construction in 1878 and was broad-gauged as part of the takeover. The BNR also included a part of the Bilaspur-Etawah State Railway which had opened in 1886. Initial railway works were at Nagpur but were moved in 1904 to Khargpur (also known as Kharagpur). The company served an area rich in coal, iron ore, manganese and limestone and thus was profitable and efficient.

The Bengal Nagpur also built what later became the Satpura lines of the South Eastern Railway and which constituted the largest network of 2-foot 6-inch gauge lines in India. Included were lines from Gondia to Nainpur and Jabalpur, from Nainpur to Chhindwara and Mandla Fort, from Gondia to Nagpur via Nagbhir, and from Itwari to Chhindwara for a total of six hundred miles. And finally the Bengal Nagpur had the Raipur Dhamtair and Rajim branch (built 1900), the Rupsa-Baripad line, the Naupada-Parlakimedi line (also opened 1900) and an isolated section of track from Purulia to Ranchi and Lohardaga (competed in 1913). A section of the Purulia-Ranchi line was broad gauged but the two ends remained 2-foot 6-inch gauge.

Oudh & Rohilkhand Railway

The Oudh & Rohilkhand Railway, originally known as the Indian Branch Railway had dabbled in both narrow and broad gauge, building an unusual 4-foot gauge line in Bengal. A broad gauge line from Bareilly through Lucknow to Moradabad was completed in 1874 and was extended to Saharanpur by 1886. It was entirely taken over by the state in 1889 and, in 1925, made part of the EIR.

Meter Gauge Lines

Lord Mayo realized that broad gauge construction was expensive and thus that, in many places, either narrow gauge roads would have to be built or the people would have to get along with nothing. He also recognized that there would be significant value in standardizing the gauge and determined that 3 foot 3 inch was appropriate, particularly as it allowed the construction of cars wide enough to carry cavalry horses two abreast. His 3 foot 3 inch choice became the meter gauge and meter gauge became one of India's standards even though the country remained on the foot-and-inch English system otherwise. By the turn of the century, India had close to ten thousand miles of meter-gauge track and operated almost fifteen hundred locomotives on it. By 1920 the locomotive count exceeded twenty-five hundred. As with the broad gauge, the locomotive fleet was heavily into 0-6-0 and 4-6-0 locomotives, these two classes comprising two-thirds of the fleet. By 1881 the state system included 1,692 miles of meter gauge and 1,366 miles of broad gauge.

The earliest examples of non-standard-gauge road construction included the Indian Branch Railway and the Indian Tramway Company. The Indian Branch Railway was built to a 4 foot gauge from Nalhati on the EIR east for twenty-seven miles to Azimganj in 1863. The line was purchased by the government in 1872 and became the Nalhati State Railway. In 1892 it was taken over by the EIR and converted to the EIR standard broad gauge. The Indian Tramway Company was formed in 1862 to build a 3-foot 6-inch gauge line from Arconum on the Madras Railway nineteen miles south to Conjeveream. Work was completed in 1865. In 1869 the line merged with the Carnatic Railway (later the South Indian Railway) and was converted to meter gauge.

Jodhpur Railways number 154 was a meter-gauge Pacific-type locomotive produced by Baldwin in the United States and shipped to India in December 1948. It had 51-inch main drivers, 15½ by 26 inch cylinders, used steam at 200 psi, and produced 18,820 pounds of tractive effort. [Author collection]

Although the meter gauge lines were initially built as local service lines and feeders for the broad gauge, they began to connect with each other and form an entirely separate, parallel system in parts of India. By 1905 the meter gauge had become a true competitor of the broad gauge. The capital cost per mile of meter gauge turned out to be half that of broad gauge and the cost of still-narrower gauges about half of that. Ton-mile operating costs, of course, were much higher.

By 1940 there were more than three thousand meter-gauge locomotives in India. The 0-6-0 and 4-6-0 wheel arrangements still predominated but they had been joined by some 4-6-2 Pacifics and some 2-8-2 Mikados (to use the American terminology). Distances on the meter gauge were relatively short, however, and loads relatively light so the additional power of the Pacifics and the Mikados was needed only in isolated instances and their numbers were relatively small.

Meter gauge construction was spread across the whole of India as shown in this map. The map shows the cities connected by the railroads, but is not a track map.

With one exception (the South Indian Railway), the meter gauge lines were all built and operated by the State. The state, however, gave the roads individual names and maintained them as independent identities.

Although meter and narrow gauge lines seemed like good ideas when they were built, since 1992 the Government of India has been converting track to the national standard broad gauge on a continuing basis, accomplishing an average of possibly a hundred miles each year. As of April 2019, the system was down to 3,200 km of meter gauge and 1,684 of narrow gauge (down from 24,153 and 5,370 respectively in 1947). Eight lines have been designated as heritage sites and will not be converted but the rest is slowly being broadened.

Many of the more significant meter-gauge lines are described in the material that follows.

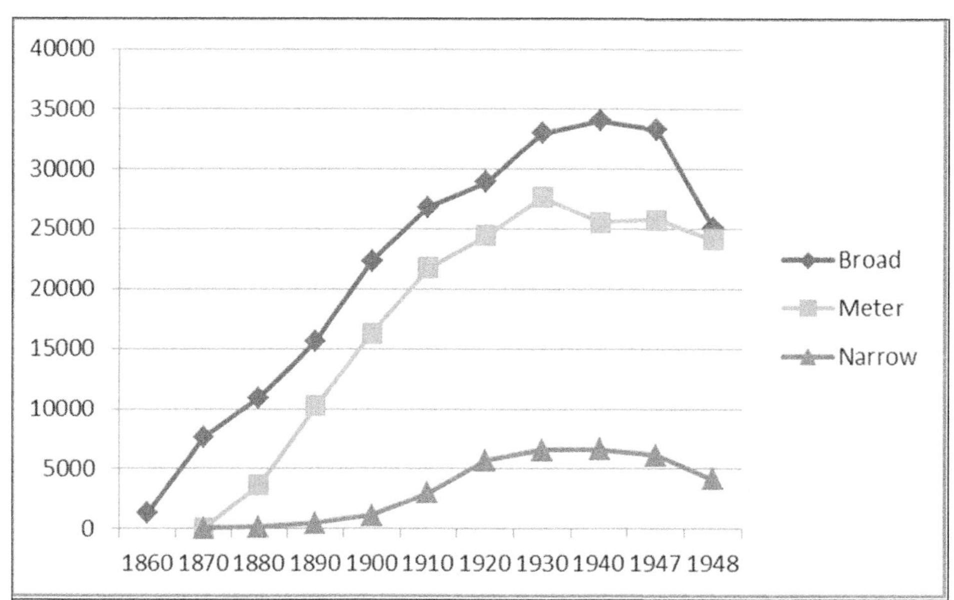

Route-kilometers of railways in India from 1860 through 1948 (after independence). The separation of Burma from India in 1937 resulted in the loss of 3,315 km of primarily meter gauge route. During World War II over a thousand km of line were taken up by the British for use elsewhere. Then, in 1947, the separation of Pakistan and Bangladesh from India resulted in the loss of another 11,198 km of mixed broad, meter gauge and narrow gauge routes in total.

Assam-Bengal Railway

The Assam-Bengal Railway was completed in 1903, running from Chittagong to Tinsukia where it connected with the Dibru-Sadiya Railway. 574 miles long, it included a branch to Gauhati and several branches to other destinations. Chittagong, now in Bangladesh east of Calcutta, was an important port city. Tinsukia was and still is in the far northeast corner of India, well along on the route to Tibet and the high mountains. The center section of the road is mountainous (although not like the Himalayas) and difficult to run through. A flood and washout in 1915 closed the line for two years and was complicated by an earthquake in the summer of 1918.

The Assam-Bengal Railway, also known as the Bengal-Assam Railway, made use of vacuum braking systems as did many Indian rail lines. Some cars had brakes and others had only pass-through pipes that carried the vacuum line on to the next car. The railway had rules about how many of these piped cars could be inserted into a train in the hill sections and how they had to be distributed in consists. The rules, at least in 1910, also specified that, since drunken coolies were known to frequently use the tracks as walking paths and were known to be careless in their habits, train crews were not to be blamed if someone was run over.

Assam Railways & Trading Company

Also known as the Dibru-Sadiya Railway, the Assam Railways & Trading Company was a short line built in the area of Dibrugarh to carry products from the local tea gardens and coal, petroleum and timber from mines and forests to the river for transportation to customers by boat. (Dibrugarh is in the northeast corner of India, more than six hundred miles from Chittagong on the Brahmaputra River.) The road was completed in 1885 and when, subsequently, the Assam-Bengal Railway built through town, it made connections with it. In 1942 it became part of the Assam-Bengal Railway and in 1945 was purchased outright by the A-B.

Bengal & North-Western Railway

The Bengal & North-Western Railway was built in northern central India starting in 1882 and opening for business in 1884. The line merged with the Tirhoot State Railway in 1890 and by 1914 had more than two thousand miles of track. In 1924 the B&NW assumed control of the Rohilkund & Kumaon Railway but the two lines continued to be operated separately. Both were purchased by the State in 1943, becoming the Oudh & Tirhut Railway and then, in 1952, being made a part of the North Eastern Railway group.

The Bengal & North-Western was the first railway in India to be built without a government guarantee.

Bengal Dooars Railway

The Bengal Dooars Railway was opened in 1893 to serve the tea industry in the northern part of the Bengal state which is at the Ganges-Brahmaputra Delta on the Bay of Bengal, today in eastern India and Bangladesh. It was taken over by the State in 1941 and became part of the Eastern Bengal Railway. A relatively short line, in its entire history it owned only twenty-three locomotives. Notably, none of its locomotives had trailing trucks and only two had pilot trucks; the rest were all either 0-6-0 or 0-8-0 designs.

Bhavnagar State Railway

The Kathiawar State Railway was built by the government from Bhavnagar a hundred miles north to Wadhwan in 1880 and was subsequently extended to other cities in the area. In 1911 the road, which the existed in several Indian states, was subdivided along state lines and the portion in Bhavnagar became the Bhavnagar State Railway. Bhavnagar is on the west shore of the Gulf of Khambhat, some two hundred miles north of Bombay. In 1948 the BSR, along with other railroads in the area, was merged into the Saurashtra Railway.

In 1915 the BSR purchased a single railcar from Motor Rail Ltd of Bedford, England. Gasoline-powered, it carried fifty passengers and remained in service as late as 1951.

Burma Railways

Although this book is about the railways of India, borders have moved over the years and both Pakistan and Myanmar (also known as Burma) today have railroads that were originally Indian. The British took control over Burma in January 1886 and it wasn't until April 1, 1937 that the British gave the nation the status of being a separate colony. British rule, however, was effectively ended by the Japanese invasion of World War II. After the war, on January 4, 1948, following a period of unrest and uncertainty, an act of the British Parliament made Burma an independent nation.

The Rangoon & Irrawaddy Valley State Railroad opened in 1877 and in 1884 it merged with the newly completed Rangoon & Sittang Valley State Railway to form the Burma State Railway. Now comprised of more than two thousand route-miles of track, the system today covers the distance between Rangoon and Mandalay and extends both south from Rangoon two hundred miles to the small town of Ye and north from Mandalay three hundred miles to Myitkyina. A branch line east from Mandalay to Lashio features eleven miles of four percent grade. Fairlie locomotives were bought in 1896 and tried out but four 0-6-6-0 mallets purchased in 1910 from the North British Locomotive Company of Glasgow were better, each being able to haul a hundred-forty-five tons up the hill. Then, in 1924, a Beyer-Peacock 2-8-0+0-8-2 Garrett was purchased. It could haul two-hundred-twenty tons and was joined by more Garretts in the following years.

Deoghur Railway

Deoghur lies two hundred miles northwest of Calcutta. The Deoghur Railway was a four-mile meter gauge system opened in 1882 by a private company. In 1911 the line was taken over by the East Indian Railway and in 1913 it was converted to the EIR's standard broad gauge.

Eastern Bengal State Railway

The Eastern Bengal State Railway was primarily a broad gauge line but it picked up a meter gauge segment with the Northern Bengal State Railway which opened in 1878 and was subsequently merged with a welter of other meter gauge lines to form the Eastern Bengal State Railway system. Included was the 2-foot 6-inch gauge Kaunia-Dharlla Railway which was converted to meter gauge in 1901 and several other lines.

Starting in 1927, a total of thirty-three 4-6-2 Pacific-types were purchased from Nasmyth, Wilson & Co. of Manchester, England and from Berliner Machinenbau AG of Berlin. Intended for passenger service, they were all given names but, as was so common in British India, they were named entirely after British aristocrats and dignitaries, completely ignoring Indian history and sensibilities.

Gaekwar's Baroda State Railway

A number of meter-gauge lines were built from Mehsana, a town in western India about three hundred miles north of Bombay. They were all owned by the Baroda Durbar (a state government). In 1933 they became the Gaekwar's Baroda State Railway but continued to be operated independently. Then, in 1949, they were ultimately merged with the Bombay, Baroda & Central India.

One segment of the railway had the distinction of being the first narrow-gauge line to be laid in British India, and also the first railway to be owned by any Princely State of India. It was operated with oxen until 1880.

Gondal Railway

The Gondal Railway was split off from the Bhavnagar State Railway in 1911 and was, at first, operated as the Porbandar State Railway but in 1936 it became the Gondal Railway and then, in 1948, a part of the Saurashtra Railway. It ran between the cities of Gondal and Porbandar.

Indian State Railways

The term Indian State Railways is a catch-all term that covers about twenty short meter-gauge lines built between 1873 and 1887 across much of India. The lines, although disconnected from each other and managed separately, were still structured as a single railway and operated under central control in many respects.

In 1874, a group of long-boilered 0-6-4T locomotives was purchased from Nasmyth Wilson of Manchester, England. Starting in 1876 they were converted into conventional 0-6-0 tender locomotives by simply cutting the frame between the boiler and rear tank, lengthening that frame, and adding an axle to make a six-wheel tender out of it.

In 1897 the Indian Government requested a group of locomotives suitable for mail service. It received a 4-4-0 design with inside cylinders. At first there were objections from the drivers about the inaccessibility of the motions but over time those objections disappeared and the locomotives became so well-liked that when they were worn out, they were replaced with near-identical duplicates.

Jaipur State Railway

The Jaipur State Railway was built between 1905 and 1907 connecting the Rajputana State Railway on its line from Agra to Ajmer with the Bombay, Baroda & Central India broad gauge. Owned by the Jaipur State, it was worked by the BB&CIR until 1936, at which time it became independent. The Jaipur State Railway became part of the Western Railway in 1951.

Jamnagar and Dwarka Railway System

The Jamnagar and Dwarka Railway System actually consisted of three separate railroads: the Jamnagar Railway (opened in 1897), an extension of it from Jamnagar to Kuranga (built in 1922), and the Okhamandal Railway, also opened in 1922. The three roads were operated as one after 1923 and in 1948 they became part of the Saurashtra Railway.

Interestingly, the J&D made several experimental attempts to design and build railcars. The first, based on a Ford four-cylinder twenty-five horsepower chassis, was built in the early 1930s and was said to be capable of moving thirty passengers when pulling a trailer. A later experiment used a thirty horsepower Ford V8 and another used a sixty horsepower Rolls Royce. The road also experimented with articulation and built a five-car train with four-wheel trucks at the joints between the cars and a single axle at each end.

Jodhpur-Bikaner Railway

Jodhpur and Bikaner are both states within India. The Jodhpur-Bikaner Railway began as the Jodhpur State Railway in 1885 but almost immediately grew, becoming a relatively large system and extending into Bikaner. In 1891 the name was changed and the line continued westward, reaching Hyderabad in 1901. In 1924 the complex was divided into separate Jodhpur and Bikaner State Railways and in 1948, as part of the partition of India, a significant portion west of Hyderabad became part of the Pakistan Western Railway. In 1949 the remaining portions of the two railways were integrated with the Indian Railways and in 1952 they became part of the Northern Railway.

Because the J-B Railway runs through desert areas, its locomotives tended to have larger tenders than others in India. This, of course, allowed the locomotives to carry more water and be less dependent on local sources. A number of them also carried shields over their valve gear as protection from blowing sand in the desert areas.

In 1924 the J-B Railway purchased five 2-8-2s from Baldwin. Equipped with bar frames and oversized fireboxes, they were intended to burn local coal which was light and friable and required significant volume to generate enough heat.

Like the Jamnagar & Dwarka, the Bikaner State Railway dabbled with the idea of a gasoline-powered rail car. Experimentation resulted in a vehicle and could carry two upper and sixty-four lower class passengers and was powered by two Ford V8 truck engines: one for each direction of travel.

Junagadh State Railway

In April of 1911, the Junagadh State Railway was split off from the Bhavnagar State Railway. It was operated as a separate entity until 1948 when it was merged into the Saurashtra Railway.

Madras & Southern Mahratta Railway

Several railroads that were built by the state between 1877 and 1879 for famine relief were taken over by the Southern Mahratta Railway in 1882. In the following years other lines were merged into the system including the Bellary Kistna State Railway, the Mysore State Railway and others. All this was reorganized in 1908, forming the Madras & Southern Mahratta Railway and including most of the original broad gauge Madras Railway. Over the following twenty years, some lines were sold to other railroads and a few joined the fold.

The line passed over the difficult Braganza Ghat with a grade of two-and-a-half percent. For service on that grade, a group of fifteen 2-6-2T locomotives were ordered in 1888 with usual axle spacing to allow maximum pulling power while staying within the allowed load of nine-and-a-half tons per axle. After receiving a dozen of the locomotives from Kitson & Company (of Leeds, England), the company found itself out of money so the last three ended up with the Southern Mahratta Railway. In 1911, they were joined on the grade by three 0-6-6-0 mallets from the North British Locomotive Company of Glasgow. Nine of the twelve 2-6-2Ts had been withdrawn from service by 1934 and the last came off in the 1950s.

Morvi Railway

The Morvi Railway was initially constructed as a 2-foot 6-inch gauge railroad by the Thakore Sahib of Morvi. While he continued to operate the line, it was converted to meter gauge in 1905 and extended in 1934. It became a part of the Saurashtra Railway in 1948 and part of the Western Railway group in 1951.

The line had a few gasoline-powered railcars built in the railway's workshops from a variety of road vehicle spare parts At least one, intended for the Maharaja, featured streamlining which was rare on a railcar in India.

Mysore State Railway

A line from Bangalore to Mysore was opened in 1882 and became part of the Southern Mahratta Railway in 1886. A second line followed in 1889. In 1919 partial operation was transferred to the government and in 1938 the transfer was completed.

Nagpur-Chhattisgarh State Railway

The Nagpur-Chhattisgarh State Railway was opened in 1882, was purchased by the Bengal-Nagpur Railway in 1887, and was converted to broad gauge in 1888.

Nizam's State Railway

The Hyderabad-Godavery Valley Railway was opened in 1900 but was owned and operated by the Nizam's Guaranteed State Railway Company. Expansions were added for almost thirty years until the line was finally purchased by the Hyderabad State in 1930 and renamed.

South Indian Railway

The South Indian Railway came into existence in 1874 as the successor to the broad gauge Great Southern of India Railway (which was changed to meter gauge) and the Carnatic Railway (which was under construction at the time). Expanding rapidly, the system was purchased by the State in 1891 but continued to be operated by South Indian Railway personnel. In 1908 the Nilgiri line was transferred from the Madras Railway to the South Indian Railway and a few South Indian lines went to the new Madras & Southern Mahratta.

The incredible Nilgiri line, completed to Coonoor in 1899, had grades as steep as eight percent. Between Mettupalayam and Coonoor, it used the Abt rack and pinion system and is, today, the only rack railroad remaining in India. Initial attempts at operation of the line were not successful as the locomotives had too little power. Only when the superintendent made a visit to Switzerland to examine the railroads there was it possible for a successful locomotive to be designed and built. The line was extended from Coonoor to Ootacamund in 1908.

The Nilgiri line was managed by the Madras Railway from its construction until it was taken over by the South Indian in 1908. It was operated with seven 0-8-2T side tank locomotives built by the Schweizerisch Locomotive Works of Winterthur, Switzerland in 1931 supplemented by five more in 1952. They were compounds, capable of working on all four cylinders on the steep rack sections of the line and as two cylinder simple expansion locomotives on the more level sections.

Eighteen miles of the SIR line south of Madras were electrified in 1931 and four B+B electric locomotives were purchased from the British firm Hawthorne, Leslie & Co. to operate on them. Interestingly, the SIR also purchased two battery tenders that could be connected to the electric locomotives so they could work non-electrified lines and yard tracks at least briefly.

Udaipur-Chitorgarh Railway

A railway connecting the cities of Udaipur and Chitorgarh was built and opened for business in 1895. The two cities, about a hundred miles apart, are both in central northern India about five hundred miles north of Bombay. Financed by the Newar Durbar, the railroad was operated by the Bombay, Baroda & Central India Railway through 1897 and then by the Durbar. In 1940 it was renamed, becoming the Mewar State Railway.

Narrow Gauge Lines

In India, the term "narrow gauge" has a slightly different meaning than it does in the USA. Where, to Americans, anything narrower than 4' 8½" is narrow gauge, in India the term relates only to railroads built to a 2½-foot or a still narrower 2-foot gauge and excludes those built to the meter gauge. And there

This is the Baldwin builder's photo of Scindia State Railway 2-8-2 number 43 which was built in December 1948 as Baldwin's construction number 74069. The locomotive is 2-foot gauge with 33" drivers, an engine weight of 66,800 pounds and a tractive force of 13,300 pounds. It is one of four identical locomotives ordered from Baldwin at that time. [Author collection]

were (and still are) a lot of them. Not all are discussed in this book.

The first narrow gauge road in India was laid down by the Gaekwar of Baroda using a 2-foot 6-inch gauge to connect the town of Dabhoi with the nearest station of the broad gauge Bombay, Baroda & Central India. Twenty miles long, it was opened in 1862 and was initially powered by bullocks. The line had been built with eighteen pound rail; three four-wheel tank locomotives were bought in 1863, each weighing about six tons, but with the small rail, the wheels quickly became grooved and the line failed. The line was re-laid with thirty pound rail in 1870, the locomotives were re-built, and the bullocks were set aside.

Following the opening of the Gaekwar's Baroda State Railway, there was a hiatus and no narrow gauge lines were brought into service until 1878 when construction began on the first of India's famous hill railroads: the 2-foot gauge Darjeeling Himalayan.

The Matheran Light Railway was constructed in 1907 and was powered by four 0-6-0T steam locomotives built by Orenstein & Koppel of Berlin. The locomotive shown here is probably at Neral, ready for a run up the hill to Matheran. It is lettered "MST" (for Matheran Steam Tramway) and carries its number just below the letters in a spot obscured by the man standing on the ground. There were, however, only the four 0-6-0T locomotives on the line (along with a single 0-4-0T) so even though we do not know which locomotive this is, we can be sure of its origin and age. [Author collection]

Service on the Darjeeling Himalayan began in 1880 on fifty-one miles of track with a ruling gradient of four percent, with places as steep as five percent, and with curves as sharp as fifty-nine foot radius. It was subsequently joined by other steep and curvy narrow gauge lines that climbed into the mountains in the west and north of India and by 1894 another nine narrow gauge railroads had begun operation.

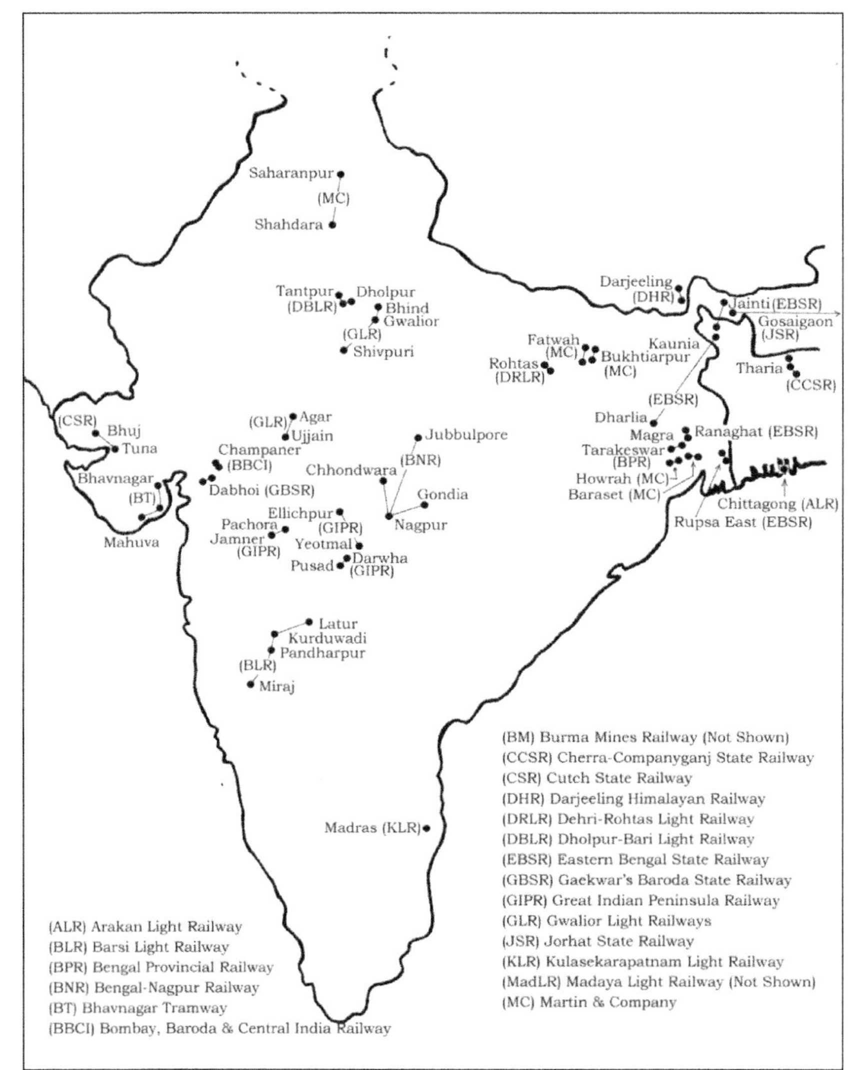

There was so much narrow gauge construction in India that it is hard to show even a representative sample on a single map. This map, therefore, includes only half. It shows the cities connected by the railroads, but should not be considered to be a track map.

In 1898 the British War Office adopted the 2-foot 6-inch gauge as its standard and the Indian Government followed suit shortly thereafter. This, in theory, allowed for some limited interchangeability of equipment but, of course, not all of the lines subsequently built adhered to the government's standard. By the first of January, 1900, there were fourteen narrow gauge railroads in operation with a total of ninety-six locomotives operating on 441 miles of 2½ foot and 256 miles of 2-foot track. Almost all of the locomotives at that point were either 4-

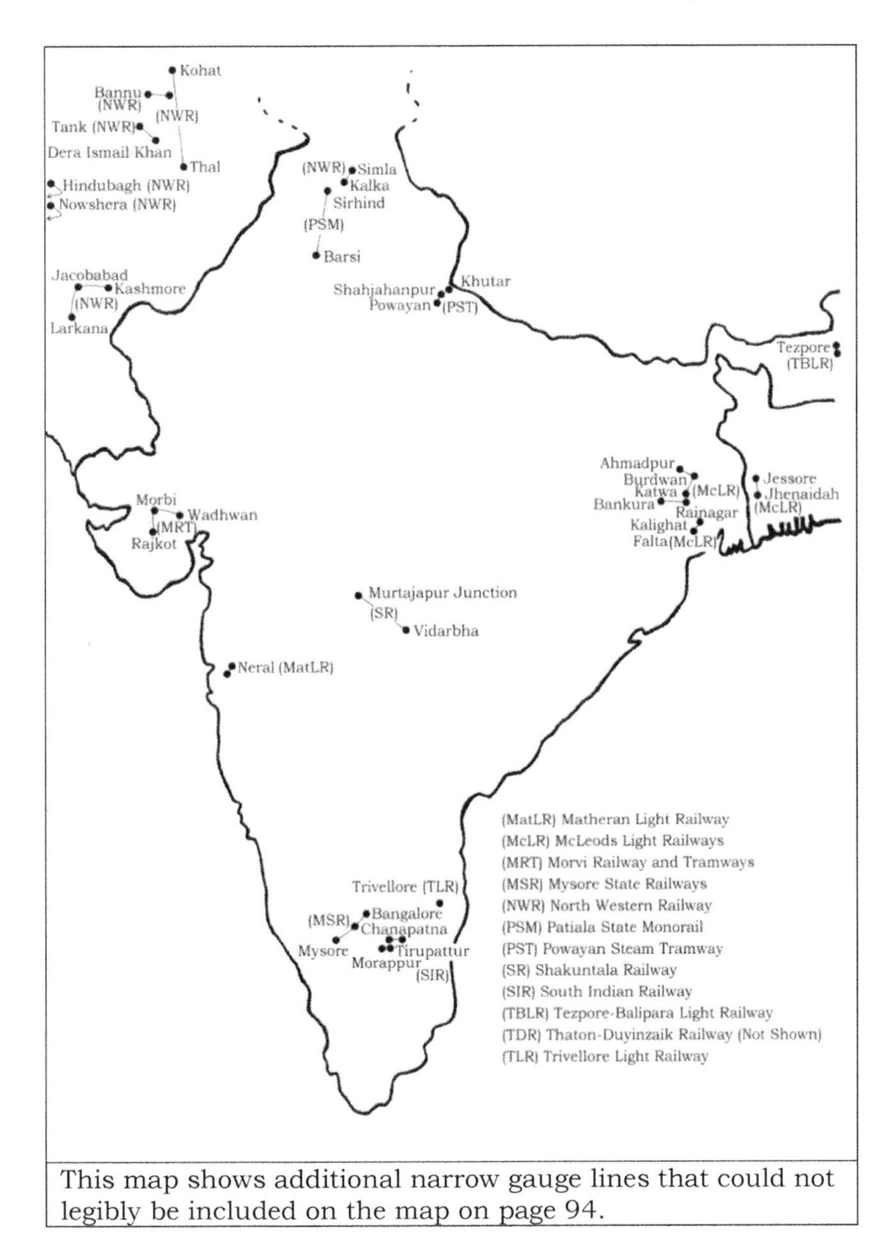

This map shows additional narrow gauge lines that could not legibly be included on the map on page 94.

or 6-coupled but one road had begun experiments with 8-coupled power and the situation was in flux.

The government, wanting traffic on its broad gauge mainlines, offered incentives to those willing to build feeder lines so, by 1918, narrow gauge track in India had reached a total of 3,431 miles and by 1940 it surpassed four thousand. By 1905 larger 2-8-4T and 4-8-4T narrow gauge locomotives had been designed and had proven successful. Standardized narrow gauge locomotives came into existence in 1925 and by 1940 there were a total of 581 in service across India. Of that number, 178 were 8-coupled, 281 were 6-coupled, and the remaining 116 were 4-coupled. Something more than half the fleet was tender locomotives but 275 were tanks.

Three 2-foot gauge lines remain in operation today: the Darjeeling Himalayan Railway (page 99), the Matheran Light Railway (page 105), and the Gwalior Light Railways (page 103).

Arakan Light Railway

The 2½ foot gauge Arakan Light Railway was formed in 1916 to take over a failed tramway that had been built to serve the workers in the rice fields and mills south of Chittagong in what is now Myanmar (Burma) but was then part of India. The line featured grades of three-and-a-half percent and two tunnels but operating expenses exceeded revenues by a substantial margin so in 1926 the Indian Government bought the line, dismantled it, and converted it and its tunnels to a roadway. The Arakan Light Railway operated the two smallest Garratts ever built by Beyer-Peacock.

Barsi Light Railway

The Barsi Light Railway was first opened in 1897, running from a town called Kurduwadi on the GIPR two hundred miles southeast of Bombay. By 1911 it had reached Latur, eighty-five miles away. A second line ran southwest to Pandharpur and eventually (by 1927) it reached Miraj for a length of a hundred-seventeen miles. The line was initially laid with thirty-five pound rail and steel ties. The majority of the early locomotives were 8-coupled (mostly 4-8-4 and 4-8-0) to keep axle loading as low as possible on the light rail. Trains ran up to three-hundred-eighteen tons which the railroad said was the equal of four-hundred-seventy-six bullock carts.

Management of the Barsi adopted the interesting position that the railroad's efficiency would be maximized when all cars and locomotives operated with a common axle-load and that axle load, given the Barsi's track, should be five tons. Cars and locomotives were subsequently designed to achieve that loading.

Pandharpur is a well-known pilgrimage town on the banks of Chandrabhaga River. It features the Vithoba Hindu Temple and attracts hundreds of thousands of pilgrims each year. In 1907 the Barsi Light Railway ran a total of a hundred-thirty-three special trains to accommodate the crowds.

As happened with so many railroads, highway competition became a problem so in 1925 two steam-powered railcars were purchased from the Sentinel Wagon Works of Shrewsbury, England. Delivery came in 1927 and, in 1940, one of the cars was still working.

By 1980 the line comprised a hundred-ninety-five route miles.

Bengal-Nagpur Railway

In the early years of the twentieth century, the Bengal-Nagpur Railway was the largest operator of narrow gauge lines in India although it owned only a portion of the lines it ran. Included were the Parlakimedi Light Railway which the Bengal-Nagpur began operating in 1902, the Mourbhanj State Railway which is began operating in 1905, and the Raipur-Dhamtari Railway which had been built as 2-foot 6-inch gauge in 1896, had been converted to 2-foot gauge in 1897 at the request of the government, and then was converted back to 2-foot 6-inch gauge in 1899 when the government changed its mind.

The Bengal-Nagpur's own lines ran to the north and east of Nagpur to places like Jubbulpore (Jabalpur), Chhindwara, Gondia, and elsewhere. The lines were built to high standards (high for India, at least) using forty and forty-one pound rail. They were worked by a relatively large stable of 4-6-2 Pacific types and 2-8-2 Mikado types with a few 2-8-4Ts and three railcars added to the mix. The twenty-eight mile 2-foot gauge Tusar-Tirodi Tramway, owned by the Central India Mining Company, was used for the movement of manganese ore. It was taken over by the Bengal-Nagpur in 1916 and was partly converted to broad gauge in 1929 with the unconverted segments dismantled between 1934 and 1936.

Bengal Provincial Railway

The thirty-two mile Bengal Provincial Railway was built between 1890 and 1895 from Taressur on the East Indian Railway northwest of Howrah, northeastwards to Magra, also on the East Indian Railway. Built to the 2-foot 6-inch gauge, it did not prove profitable and post-war losses caused its closure in 1956.

Bhavnagar Tramway

In India, the concept of a tramway, as opposed to a railway, is similar in some respects to a private, as opposed to a common carrier in the US. That is, lines that qualified as tramways were exempted from some regulation and were not required to keep some records and file some otherwise mandatory reports. The Bhavnagar Tramway, although sixty-seven miles long, qualified, in part, because it was built with only thirty pound rail and was thus greatly limited in the loads it could carry. A special series of light 4-8-0 locomotives that rode on drivers only twenty-eight inches in diameter and had axle loads of only five tons operated on the line.

Bombay, Baroda & Central India Railway

In addition to its broad gauge and meter gauge lines, the Bombay, Baroda & Central India took over the 2-foot 6-inch gauge Champaner-Shivrajpur Light Railway in 1922. The line had been built by the Gaekwar of Baroda to haul manganese ore in 1911 and had been taken over by the Guzetrat Railway in 1915.

Burma Mines Railway

The Burma Mines Corporation built a 2-foot gauge railway to haul lead ore from the mines at Bawdwin 51 miles to Manpwe on the meter gauge Burma Railway with the goal of being able to move the ore on to the company's smelter in Mandalay. Based on a mixture of forty-one pound and thirty pound rail, the line had a ruling grade of 3.7% and curves as sharp as forty-six degrees. When it was opened in 1910, consideration was given to offering passenger service but that never materialized. The mine, itself, was an old Chinese silver mine that had been stripped of silver and abandoned but had been found to contain significant quantities of lead. What is surprising is that, given the density and weight of lead ore and the distance which it had to be hauled, that the company did not spend the money to build a meter gauge line and thus avoid the need for transfer at Manpwe. The reason is probably split between the rough terrain which meant that a broader gauge road would have been more expensive to build, and the low cost of labor which made the Manpwe transfer less onerous.

Cherra-Companyganj State Railway

The 2-foot 6-inch gauge Cherra-Companyganj State Railway was built beginning in 1884 with the goal of providing access to the Provincial capital from Calcutta. Over a distance of about fifteen track miles the road ran from Cherrapunji at elevation 4286 feet to Taria at 1086 feet and from there to Companyganj at forty-two feet. The route required an average grade of about 5.4% which certainly would have meant stretches of eight percenbt or more had it been built that way. Instead the railroad climbed only a little more than a thousand feet in its first ten miles and was then faced with a climb of thirty-six hundred feet over the next three. The plans called for a series of seven rope-hauled inclines to conquer the steepest parts and then another half-dozen miles of conventional railroad to reach Cherrapunji. It was built and opened for service in 1886 but the inclines never worked properly so they and the section to Cherrapunji were dismantled starting in 1891. An earthquake in 1897 and flooding in 1899 brought additional challenges and the road was finally abandoned in 1901.

Cutch State Railway

The Maharaja Maha Raio Sahib of Cutch had a 2-foot 6-inch gauge railway built from the port of Tuna on the Gulf of Cutch on the western side of India near what is now the Pakistan border north to Anjar. It opened for service in 1905 and was extended to the state capitol at Bhuj in 1908 making it just under thirty-seven miles long. In subsequent years, additional track was added running east from Anjar and by 1940 more than three hundred thousand passengers were being carried annually.

The Cutch State Railway operated an interesting railcar purchased in 1910 from McEwan Pratt & Company of Wickford, England. Intended as a shooting car for the Maharaja's hunting expeditions and powered by a small internal steam engine, it had a pair of center drive wheels with a 4-wheel truck at each end.

Darjeeling Himalayan Railway

The Darjeeling Himalayan Railway was and is a 2-foot gauge line that runs from Siliguri where there is a connection with the broad gauge Assam-Bengal Railway to Darjeeling in the Himalayas. It also has branch lines to Kishanganj in the rice paddies of the Ganges plain and to Gielle Khola in a canyon on the Teesta River. At Kishangnj there is a connection with the Assam-Bengal's meter-gauge line.

The British Army had built a sanatorium for its soldiers in the cooler mountain air at Darjeeling. Getting there required transportation so work began on the railroad in 1879 and it was completed in 1881. Today, the Darjeeling Himalayan continues to do a significant business with tourists who want to see the spectacular scenery and with Indian citizens who want to escape the summer heat of the plains. The fifty-one mile railroad accomplishes seven thousand feet of climb without tunneling but with four loops and five switchbacks, one of the loops having a radius of only sixty feet. The ruling grade from Siliguri to Sukna, where the hill actually starts, is only 0.3% but from Sukna to the summit at Ghum, the average grade is 3.3%.

At one point the road owned an aerial tramway that ran from Rilli on the Gielle Khola line some seven miles to Kalipong. While the line to Darjeeling continues to handle significant numbers of passengers, most of the traffic on the SIliguri-Kishanganj line is freight consisting of tea, rice and jute.

Laid with fifty pound steel rail, the line allowed a speed of only twelve miles per hour. At Sukna, seven miles from Siliguri, most trains were split into three or four car sections for the climb up the steep part of the railroad. Locomotives were often crewed by six: an engineer, a fireman, two coal passers/breakers, and two additional brakemen who rode the front pilot beam, ready to drop sand on the rails if the locomotive slips.

The locomotives had steam brakes but the cars had only mechanical ones. Nevertheless, despite relatively frequent minor derailments, the safety record of the line was good. Every locomotive carried re-railing equipment and the crews generally made short work of whatever happened.

Near the bottom of the line it passed through a forested area that was home to a variety of wild animals including tigers, leopards, buffalo, hogs, wolves and elephants. At one point in the early years of operation, a herd of wild elephants disrupted operations on the line and forced trains to return to Sukna to wait for the invaders to leave.

The trains carried no diners so there was usually a lunch stop at Kurseog where there were separate European, Hindu and Muslim refreshment rooms. Although there was a turntable at Darjeeling, the locomotives were designed for two-way operation and they normally made the return journey in reverse.

The Darjeeling Himalayan Railway operated primarily with short-wheelbase 0-4-0 locomotives made necessary by the tight curvature on its lines. It did, however, own two small 4-6-2 Pacifics which were used primarily in the plains at the bottom of the mountains and on the branch to Kishanganj. Unfortunately, the road's shops were at Tindharia, eighteen miles from Siliguri and on the other side of some curves that ultimately proved to be too sharp for the Pacifics so they were serviced using makeshift methods on a side track at the bottom of the hill.

The road had one solitary Garrett and, in 1942, bought its first diesel which was not terribly successful on the hill section. Also at some point in the late 1930s, the line selected one of its 0-4-0 hill locomotives and applied a streamlined sheath to it. At twelve miles an hour, streamlining is certainly superfluous but it was the trendy thing to do so the road did it.

The 0-4-0+0-4-0 Garret was ordered in 1910 from Beyer, Peacock & Company and was delivered in 1911. Unfortunately, it had been designed with only a single reversing mechanism and that made it hard for the engineers to balance the force exerted by the front truck with that by the rear so the locomotive was slippery. Modifications and experiments were made and the locomotive lasted on the line until 1954 but was not much used and there were no further experiments with articulation.

A rail car built by Motor Rail Ltd of Bedford, England in 1920 carried nine passengers and was able to make the run from Siliguri to Darjeeling in an hour and a half less than the regular train.

Dehri-Rohtas Light Railway and Dwara-Therria Light Railway

The Dehri-Rohtas Light Railway was originally built in 1907 as a 2-foot 6-inch gauge tramway running twenty-four miles from Rohtas to Dehri-on-Sone where it made a connection with the East Indian Railway main line. In 1909, however, the Dwara-Therria Light Railway became available when its promoter died and, to make it possible to take over that road, the Octavius Steel Company (of Calcutta), owner of the Dehri-Rohtas line, upgraded it to the status of a railway. By 1914 the two lines were handling fifty thousand passengers and ninety thousand tons of freight annually. They were ultimately worked by a stable of nine 6-coupled tank locomotives of which seven were 0-6-2T, one 0-6-0T and one 0-6-4T. The 0-6-0T, which was the road's number 4, had originally been built for a Russian 750mm gauge road but had ended up in India.

Dholpur-Bari Light Railway

The 2-foot 6-inch gauge Dholpur-Bari Light Railway was built in 1908 by the Maharaj Rana of Dholpur in central northern India south of Delhi. It initially went only to Bari, a distance of about twenty miles but was extended an additional eighteen miles to Tantpur in 1914 and another twenty from Bari to Sirmuttra by 1929. The road was used mostly to haul stone, originally for the building of New Delhi.

Eastern Bengal State Railway

In addition to its broad and meter gauge lines (see page 87), the Eastern Bengal State Railway operated 2-foot 6-inch gauge lines. Included were the Kaunoia-Dharlia State Railway (1884 Kaunia to the Brahmaputra river and to Dharlla), the Cooch Behar State Railway (1901 Gitaldaha north to Jainti), the Ranaghat-Krishnagar Light Railway (1899 Ranaghat to Krishnagar), and the Khulna-Bagerhat Railway (1918 Rupsa East to Bagerhat). None of these roads were long – the Ranaghat-Krishnagar had only twenty miles of track – but some lasted a long time – the Ranaghat-Krishnagar was not torn up until the 1980s.

Small and narrow railroads are generally operated with small locomotives. As an example, the Ranaghat-Krishnagar Light Railway ran a class of 2-4-0T locomotives with tiny 24½-inch drivers and even smaller sixteen-inch pony wheels.

Gaekwar's Baroda State Railway

Between 1861 and 1862 a twenty-mile 2-foot 6-inch gauge line was built from Dabhoi to Miyagam on the Bombay, Baroda & Central India broad gauge line. Owned by the Gaekwar, the line was at first worked by bullocks but in 1863 three 0-4-0T tank locomotives were purchased. They turned out to be unusable, however, because the decision had been made to build the road with only 13-pound rail and it could not support their weight. The bullocks were returned to service and in 1871 work began on relaying the line with new thirty pound rail. By 1873 steam was working, the line was fully opened and operations was taken over by the BB&CIR. Starting in 1879, extensions and branches were built, one from Bilimora to Wabhai, a second from Kosamba to Umarpada, and a third near Petlad. In 1921 the State of Baroda took over the working of all these lines from the BB&CIR and the name was changed becoming Gaekwar's Baroda State Railway.

The Dabhoi-Miyagram segment of the railway was the first narrow gauge to be built in India. It was followed by a 4 foot gauge section of the East Indian Railway between Halhati and Azimganj in 1963 but that section did not stay narrow.

By 1923, five lines, all radiating from Dabhoi, totaled two-hundred-fifteen miles of route. The central locomotive repair shop in Dabhoi had forty tracks.

The earliest locomotives on the line had been built by W G Bagnall, Ltd of Stafford; the passenger and freight cars used were built locally in India. Also among the locomotives operated were seven 0-6-2 tender locomotives purchased from Kitson & Company (of Leeds, England) in two groups: 1902 and 1909. They had unusual Hawthorn-Kitson valve gear with side sheeting to protect the valves from road debris and dust. Two of the seven ultimately went to other lines but five served until being withdrawn in 1950s.

In 1925 the line purchased a twenty horsepower inspection car from the Drewery Car Company of London and in 1932, reacting to competition from the highways, it purchased four eighty horsepower gas-powered railcars from Armstrong Whitworth & Company of Newcastle-upon-Tyne, England.

Great Indian Peninsula Railway

Like many of the broad gauge railways, the Great Indian Peninsula Railway operated its share of narrow gauge feeder roads: the Central Provinces Railway (1915 Ellichpur to Yeotmal), the Darwha Pusad Railway (1931 Darwha to Pusad), the Pachora-Jamner Railway (1919 Pachora to Jamner), and others. All were 2-foot 6-inch gauge.

Gwalior Light Railways

In the early 1890s the Maharaja Madhava Rao Scindia built a short 2-foot gauge railway on the grounds of his palace in Gwalior. The line was built with twenty pound rail but apparently was successful because he had it extended to the Morar residence, his hunting lodge, and a state farm. Having proved the concept to his satisfaction, the Maharaja then had his lines extended and opened to the public. Now with thirty pound rail, the new lines reached fifty miles northeast to Bhind (completed 1899), seventy miles southwest to Shipuri (completed 1899) and a hundred-twenty miles west to Shopur Kalan (completed 1909). An isolated line two-hundred-forty miles southwest from Gwalior ran forty miles from Agar to Ujjain and was completed in 1932. The Maharaja's lines were operated by the Great Indian Peninsula Railway starting in 1900 but from 1913 operations were taken over by the Durbar and in 1942 the road was renamed the Scindia State Railway while ownership was passed to the Central Railway.

In 1904 the Maharaja purchased a steam railcar for his private use but it suffered excessive vibration and was little used. Later railcars purchased in 1908, 1910, 1914 and 1934 were more successful.

Jorhat State Railway

Begun as the Kokilamukh State Railway and intended to serve the local tea farms, what became the 2-foot gauge Jorhat State Railway was opened in 1887. In 1915 it became the Jorhat Provincial Railway and was taken over by the Indian Government in 1937. Part of it was subsequently converted to meter gauge and the rest dismantled.

Kulasekarapatnam Light Railway

This 2-foot gauge system, possibly most distinctive for the complexity of its name, was built for the East India Distilleries and Sugar Factories of Madras. In 1914 it was opened to the public and, starting in 1918, several railcars came into use that may have been truck conversions. The line was closed in 1940.

Madaya Light Railway

The 2-foot 6-inch gauge Madaya Light Railway ran north from Mandalay, Burma eight miles to Toungbyon, opening in 1912. Completion to Madaya, another eight miles, came about in 1917 but the company went into voluntary liquidation in 1919. In 1923 its remains were purchased by the Burmese Government and taken over by the Burma Railways Company. In 1927 it was closed and replaced by a new meter gauge line.

Martin & Company

Martin & Company, a Calcutta business firm, took over the management of the Bengal Iron and Steel Co in 1889. The firm dealt with jute mills and collieries in the Bengal state north of Calcutta and had other business interests, one of which was the operation and management of several narrow gauge railways. The 2-foot gauge Howrah-Amta and Hoerah-Sheakhala Light Railways were opened in 1898. The Arrah-Sasaram Light Railway, the Futwah-Islampur Light Railway, the Baraset-Basirhat Light Railway and the Bukhtiarpur-Bihar Light Railway all acted as feeders to the East Indian Railway. The Shahdara-Saharanpur Light Railway opened in 1907 near Delhi and was ninety-two miles long. All but the first two named lines were 2-foot 6-inch gauge.

A 55hp diesel railcar was purchased in 1938 by the Baraset-Basirhat line from Walford Transport of Calcutta. It had a four-speed gearbox and chain drive.

Matheran Light Railway

The Matheran Light Railway was constructed in 1907 as a private enterprise by Sir Abdul Hussein Adamjee Peerbhoy at a cost to him in Rupees of the equivalent of $24,000 US (which is about $650,000 in 2020 dollars). Built to conquer the hills surrounding Matheran, a popular vacation spot twenty-five miles east of Bombay in the mountains, it ran from Neral to Matheran with a 2-foot gauge and a ruling grade of five percent which kept trains short and light. The road was operated by the Great Indian Peninsula Railway until 1926 at which point the company took over. An eight-seat gasoline railcar was purchased in 1909 and a second, fourteen-seat car in 1927. Both of the railcars were powered by Dodge gas engines and had chain drives.

At one point, construction of the railway required the blasting and removal of ancient rock to make way for the rails. When the blasts were set off, however, hundreds of snakes crept from their hiding places; the workmen's superstitions prevented them from capturing or killing the snakes so they represented an unusual problem. Finally the company offered a reward of 1 Rupee for each snake killed. That incentive overrode the superstitions and solved the problem.

The Matheran Light Railway had four 0-6-0T locomotives built by Orenstein & Koppel in 1907. Their leading and trailing axles were equipped with Kleiner flotation devices, reducing the length of the rigid wheelbase to a minimum and allowing the locomotives to work the line's sharp curvature.

McLeods Light Railways

The 2-foot 6-inch gauge Jessore-Jhendah Railway was built in 1913 but its early management failed to properly maintain it so it was taken over by McLeod & Company of Calcutta in 1915. McLeod was unable to solve the road's problems so it went into liquidation in 1924, was purchased, went into liquidation a second time in 1933, and was finally permanently closed in 1936.

McLeod also managed several other, more successful 2-foot 6-inch gauge roads in the Bengal area: the Burdwan-Katwa line of 1915, the Ahmadpur-Katwa line of 1917, the Bankura-Damoodar River Railway of 1917 and the Kalighat-Falta line of 1917. All were guaranteed by the government to return at least three-and-a-half percent and all operated well into the 1940s.

Highway competition became an issue as it was on so many railroads. One author quotes an official of the Kalighat-Falta line as saying, "If a train is about the start the fares [on competing buses] are slightly lower than those of the railway, otherwise the fares are higher." Since highway travel didn't involve predefined departure times, the railroad couldn't reciprocate.

The Kalighat-Falta line was closed in the 1970s and two other lines were taken over by the government: the Bankura-Damoodar River by the South Eastern Railway and the Ahmadpur-Katwa by the Eastern Railway.

Morvi Railway and Tramways

The Morvi Railway was built by the Thakore Sahib of Morvi to a 2-foot 6-inch gauge connecting the towns of Wadhwan, Morvi and Rajkot. It opened in 1890 but starting in 1905 piecemeal conversion to meter gauge was begun. As the conversion made equipment available, tramway feeder lines were built to the original 2-foot 6-inch gauge.

The first trackage of the Morvi Railway was laid with patent steel tramway rails from the Kerr Stewart & Company of Stoke-on-Trent, England. They were an incredibly light 19 pounds per yard and would support only an axle loading of three-and-a-half tons. New rail of twenty-nine pound weight was soon installed and locomotive weights grew to suit. Two gasoline-powered locomotives were purchased: one a twelve horsepower 0-4-0 in 1905 from Kerr Stewart and the other a thirty horsepower 0-4-0 in 1910 from Nasmyth, Wilson & Company of Manchester, England. How long they lasted and how much they were actually able to accomplish is no longer known.

Mysore State Railways

The Mysore State Railways consisted of three lines: the Bowringpet-Kolar Railway (2-foot 6-inch gauge opened in 1913) which became the Kolar District Railway after a 1916 expansion; the Bangalore-Chik Ballapur Light Railway (2-foot 6-inch gauge opened in stages by 1918), and the Tarikere-Narasimharajapura Tramway (2-foot gauge opened in 1917). All ran in the area of Bangalore in southern India.

The Bowringpet-Kolar line served a gold mine at Kolar.

North Western Railway

The North Western was a major operator of narrow gauge lines with something like fourteen of them under its control. Over the years, these fourteen lines were operated by a hundred-sixty 2-foot 6-inch gauge locomotives, sixty-three 2-foot gauge locomotives, and sixteen 2-foot 6-inch gauge railcars, three of which were steam powered, one diesel and the rest gasoline.

The 2-foot 6-inch gauge railways were:

- The Nowshera-Dargai State Railway, forty miles long, opened in 1901 and converted to broad gauge in 1922.
- The Kushalgarh-Kohat-Thal Railway, opened in 1902 and extended in 1903 for a total of ninety-one miles. Its initial connection with the North Western was at Khushalgarh via a ropeway across the Indus River but this was taken down after an accident in 1903. The Indus was bridged and the line was broad-gauged in 1908.
- The Kalka-Simla Railway, originally built as 2-foot gauge but changed to 2-foot 6-inch gauge in 1901. Sixty miles long, with a hundred-three tunnels and with grades as steep as three percent, it was completed in 1903, became state property in 1906, and was taken over by the North Western in 1907.
- The Bhaganwalla Colliery, built north of Malakwal. This short line never achieved its goals and was closed in 1899.
- The Kalabagh-Bannu (Trans Indus) Railway, eighty-nine miles long, opened in 1913. The line long depended on a wagon ferry across the Indus River but finally, in 1931, a bridge was completed. A branch from Lake Marwat to Tank had grades as steep as 2.2%.
- The Jacobabad-Kashmore Railway, seventy-six miles long, opened in 1914. It was converted to broad gauge in 1956.
- The Marala Timber Depot Railway ran four miles from the timber depot to the River Chenab.
- The Khanai-Hindubagh Railway, also known as the Zhob Valley Railway was originally built to serve the mines operated by the Baluchistan Chrome Company. It reached an altitude of 7,221 feet which was the highest point on the North Western. First opened in 1917 it was incorporated into the North Western in 1921 and later was extended to a total length of a hundred-seventy-four miles.
- The Larkana-Jacobabad Railway was constructed by the Sind Railway, was fifty-three miles long, and was opened in 1923. The North Western operat-

ed it until 1939 at which point the state assumed ownership and (in 1940) converted it to broad gauge.

- The Dhilwan Creosoting Plant made railroad ties and was thus an important supplier of the North Western. The plant had an extensive internal railway that the North Western operated at least through the 1930s.
- The Kangra Valley Railway, a hundred-three miles long, featured two tunnels, fifty-three bridges with more than a forty-foot span, grades up to four percent, and was opened in 1929. It was dismantled in 1942 but then rails were reinstalled (with minor changes) and the line was reopened in 1976.

The 2-foot gauge railways were:

- The Ferozepore Steam Tramway, six and three-quarter miles long, was opened in 1885 and closed in 1888. It ran across a boat bridge over the Sutlej River.
- The Dandot Light Railway, six miles long, was fully opened by 1895 and included several wire rope inclines. It was built to serve the Dandot Colliery.
- The Military Reserve Railway, forty-two miles long from Dera Ismail Khan on the Indus River to Tank on the Kalabagh-Bannu Railway. Built with war surplus materials, it was opened in 1920 and was equipped with fifty Baldwin-built 600mm gauge 4-6-0T locomotives that were also war surplus. (600mm is 23.6 inches, probably close enough to two feet that the locomotives could run without gauge conversion.) The line was closed in 1928 and the locomotives were dispersed.

There are three true mountain railroads in India today: the relatively famous Darjeeling-Himalayan, the Nilgiri and the Kalka-Simla. The last of these three, the 30-inch Kalka-Simla, is part of the North Western system and is the only one of the three designed for conventional rod locomotives. It connects Kalka at 2,141 feet of altitude with Simla, sixty miles away, at an altitude of 7,246 feet. Simla (also known as Shimla) is a place of recreation and has been the summer seat of several governments, it became especially popular after the railroad was completed in 1903. There are a hundred-three tunnels on the line and the ruling gradient is three-and-a-quarter percent. The line is not wholly curved but much of it is with the sharpest curve laid out at a hundred-nineteen foot radius. Oddly, there is only one girder bridge and one steel trestle viaduct, all of the remaining bridgework being of stone. There are no branches and passing tracks exist only at the twenty intermediate stations.

The longest tunnel on the Kalka-Simla is number thirty-three, the Barog Tunnel (3,752 feet long) which was designed by a British Colonel named Barog. As was often done, crews began digging from both ends but when they got to the halfway point, the two headings didn't meet; Barog's calculations had been wrong. A second tunnel was subsequently dug under a different engineer and this time the headings met properly. The original tunnel is still there but the second one is the one that is used. Barog, it is said, rode into his failed tunnel, committed suicide, and his ghost is still there.

Several other ghost stories are attached to the old, unused Barog Tunnel: a werewolf is said to have been the cause of Barog's miscalculations and is said to still populate the area; a witch clad in white entices people into the tunnel from which they never emerge; a pregnant woman in black clutching a baby was killed by a motorist near the tunnel and she is sometimes seen there; and finally, a signalman with a green lantern appears from time to time luring people into the tunnel. Like the white witch, those who accept his invitation are never seen again.

By the 1830s, Simla had already developed as a major base for the British. It became the summer capital of British India in 1864, and also the Headquarters of the British army in India. The Kalka-Simla Railway was built to connect Simla, the summer capital of India during the British Raj, with the Indian rail system. It is believed that Baba Bhalkhu a local saint, who possessed some supernatural engineering skills, helped the British engineers in laying down this track.

The first two steam locomotives that worked on Kalka-Simla Railway were from Sharp, Stewart and Company of Glasgow, built in 1900 & 1902 respectively. They were soon joined by ten 0-4-2Ts (also by Sharp Stewart) and by 1910, thirty K class 2-6-2Ts (by North British Locomotive) were on the line. Locomotive number KC-520, one of the first of the 2-6-2Ts, built in 1905, is still surviving.

The first cars built for Kalka-Simla Railway in 1903 were small four-wheelers measuring seventeen feet from buffer to buffer. Many had very long service lives and several can still be seen in museums. Eight-wheel bogie coaches eventually appeared on the line and, interestingly, they featured aluminum roofs in an early attempt to reduce dead weight. The ultimate in first-class luxury travel of the Kalka-Simla was diesel-electric railcar number 14 that featured very large windows to give an uninterrupted view of the incredible scenery as the train climbed the track. The headlight on 14 was built to swivel with the track curvature to provide a better view of the track for the crew. There were turntables at each end of the KSR but the steam locomotives didn't use them; they were for use by rail cars and other vehicles that didn't easily travel in reverse.

The earliest rail motor cars on Kalka-Simla were petrol driven supplied by the Drewery Car Co. Ltd of London. The four rail motor cars (Nos 1, 2, 3 and 4) working on this section were built in 1927 and repowered in 2001 with Leyland engines. Altogether, twelve of the North Western's sixteen railcars ran on the Kalka-Simla, larger and later ones handling as many as thirty-six passengers. Two of them had unusual 2-4-2 wheel arrangements.

Diesel traction was introduced on the Kalka-Simla in 1956 with the procurement of 5DZ (Later ZDM-1) class locomotives built by the Arnold Jung Lokomotivfabrik of Germany. By the 1970s, the Kalka-Simla had completely replaced its steam locomotives with diesel-hydraulics.

The Kalka-Simla became a Unesco World Heritage Site in 2008.

Patiala State Monorail

Possibly the ultimate in narrow gauge railroading is represented by the 0-foot gauge monorail. The Patiala State Monorail was first built in 1906 to connect Sirhind station on North Western Railway, and the town of Barsi. The Ewing patent monorail system was used and a single rail was laid on the ground. Cars ran on that rail, initially pulled by oxen and mules (of which the government had a surplus that needed utilization). Although the rail carried the bulk of the load, the cars all had a balancing wheel on one side. That wheel ran on what amounted to a dirt road beside the rail. Eventually, however, a steam locomotive design was approved and four locomotives were built by Orenstein & Koppel of Berlin and delivered in 1909. They were, interestingly 0-3-0 locomotives (that designation ignoring the balance wheel on one side). One of the locomotives and one of the cars still exist at the National Rail Museum in New Delhi.

Powayan Steam Tramway

The Powayan Steam Tramway was a 2-foot 6-inch gauge line that ran from Shahjahanpur on the Oudh & Rohilkhand Railway to Powatyan, Khotar, and Mailani where it met the meter gauge Rohilkund & Kumaon. Extending forty miles, it was completed in 1894 and earned its keep hauling fuel for Shahjahanpur and the Rosa sugar factory. For some years, reminiscent of similar restrictions in England, the train had to follow a man carrying a red flag when it moved through Powyan but that rule was eventually dropped. The Rohilkund & Kumaon took over operations in 1900 and management in 1907. In 1918, as part of the war effort, the road was entirely commandeered by the government. It was closed and its rolling stock dispersed in 1921.

Shakuntala Railway

The 2-foot 6-inch gauge Shakuntala Railway was built privately by a British firm in 1857 to carry cotton twenty-five miles from Vidarbha to Murtajapur Junction on the broad gauge. From the junction, the cotton would then be hauled by the GIPR to Bombay and from there shipped by water to England. Interestingly, the Shakuntala Railway still exists as a separate entity. It was not included in the master nationalization plan, according to some, simply because it was forgotten. Today, the Shakuntala is run by the Central Railway with rent amounting to fifty-five percent of passenger revenue annually paid to its owners. It was steam-powered until 1995 when its class ZD 4-6-2 steam engine, built in Manchester in 1921, was finally retired.

South Indian Railway

The South Indian Railway, a meter gauge road, took over operations of two 2-foot 6-inch roads from the Madras Railway in 1907. The Tirupattur-Krishnagiri Railway had opened in 1905 and the Morappur-Dharmapuri Railway in 1906. Both were famine protection lines owned by the Government. The Tirupattur-Krishnagiri operated with a group of 2-8-4T locomotives but found that the line's curves were so sharp that the locomotives were damaging the track. The solution, it was found, was to operate the locomotives in reverse because the 4-wheel trailing truck did a better job of steering the locomotive than did the 2-wheel pilot truck.

Tezpore-Balipara Light Railway

The 2-foot 6-inch gauge Tezpore-Balipara Light Railway was completed in 1895 primarily to serve the local tea gardens. It ran on thirty-pound flat-bottomed steel rail and was relatively well built. In 1907, 4,203 tons of tea were handled. The line used semi-open passenger cars that resembled San Francisco's cable cars in appearance; the closed half of the car was reserved for first class passengers while everyone else sat in the open half exposed to the sun and rain.

Thaton-Duyinzaik Railway

The Thaton-Duyinzaik Railway, which is now in Burma, was privately built and opened in 1885. Laid to the 2-foot 6-inch gauge, it ran eight miles along a jungle road to a boat landing in Duyinzaik. In 1900 the Irrawaddy Flotilla Company took over the line and in 1907, when the meter gauge Burma Railways reached Thaton, it closed.

Trivellore Light Railway

The Trivellore Light Railway was a 2-foot gauge line that ran a short two miles from the Trivellore railway station to the local temple. Built in 1904, it operated with steam power until 1939.

Bibliography

Books

- ___, Smithsonian Train; The Definitive Visual History, Dorling Kindersley, 2014
- Aklekar, Rajendra B, *Short History of Indian Railways*, Rupa Publications, 2019
- Armytage, WHG, *A Social History of Engineering*, Faber & Faber, 1961
- Bagwell, Philip S, The Transport Revolution from 1770, Harper & Row, 1974
- Berridge, P S A, *Couplings to the Khyber: The Story of the North Western Railway*, Latimer Trend & Co., 1969
- Bhandari, R R, *Locomotives in Steam*, Indian Railways, 1981
- Chakravarti, A K, Railways for Developing Countries, Chetana Publications, 1982
- Coleman, Terry, *The Railway Navvies*, Penguin Books 1968
- Hansen, Peter A (Ed.), *After Promontory*, Indiana Univ. Press, 2019
- Hughes, Hugh, *Indian Locomotives*, Continental Railway Circle, 1990-96
- Hughes, Hugh, *Steam in India*, D Bradford Barton (England) 1976
- Huddleston, G, *History of the East Indian Railway*, Calcutta, Thacker Spink & Co 1906
- Kerr, Ian J, *Building the Railways of the Raj 1850-1900*, Oxford Univ. Press, 1997
- Kerr, Ian J, *Engines of Change*, Praeger Publishers, 2007
- Kipling, Rudyard, The Man Who Would Be King, Oxford Univ. Press, 1987
- Kumar, Dharma (Ed), *The Cambridge Economic History of India*, vol. 2 1757-1986, Cambridge University Press, 1983
- O'Brien, Patrick, *The New Economic History of the Railways*, St. Martin's Press, 1977
- Orwell, George, The Road to Wigan Pier, Harcourt Books, 1958
- Prakash, Dileep, *Whistling Steam*, Roli Books, 2002
- Sahni, J N, *Indian Railways One Hundred Years 1853 to 1953*, Government of India, Ministry of Railways, 1953
- Satow, Michael and Ray Desmond, *Railways of the Raj*, New York University Press, 1980
- Searight, Sarah, *Steaming East*, The Bodley Head, 1991

- Twain, Mark, *Following the Equator*, American Publishing Co, 1897
- Westwood, J N, *Railways of India*, David & Charles, 1974
- Weld, William Ernest, India's Demand for Transportation, AMS Press, 1968
- White, Richard, *Railroaded*, W W Norton, 2011

Articles

- ___ (various authors), *Developing Railways* in Overseas Railways, 1964
- Bhalla, G P, *Eastern Railway of India* in Overseas Railways, 1964
- Ganguli, B C, *North-East Frontier Railway of India* in Overseas Railways, 1964
- Khandelwal, G D, *South Eastern Railway* in Overseas Railways, 1964
- Krieg, Allan D, *The Darjeeling Himalayan* in Trains Magazine, 1/1946
- Lall, Ratan, *The Central Railway of India* in Overseas Railways, 1964
- Lehmann, Fritz, *India is Still Building Steam Power*, in Railroad Magazine, 7/1967
- Lehmann, Fritz, *India Has Over 9,000 Steamers*, in Railroad Magazine, 7/1972
- Marre, Louis A., *The American Railfan in Hindustan*, in Trains Magazine, 2/1984
- Morgan, David P, *The Best Travel Experience in the Whole of India*, in Trains Magazine 7/1961
- Murthy, O S, *The Western Railway of India* in Overseas Railways, 1964
- Shaw, Robert B, *Who Operates the Largest*, in Trains Magazine 3/1968
- Singh, H D, *Southern Railway of India* in Overseas Railways, 1964
- Singh, Harbans, *The Northern Railway of India* in Overseas Railways, 1964

Web Sites

- artsandculture.google.com
- en.wikipedia.org/wiki/Indian_Railways
- en.wikipedia.org/wiki/Project_Unigauge
- indianrailways.gov.in
- nrmindia.com
- nr.indianrailways.gov.in

Index

Printed in Great Britain
by Amazon